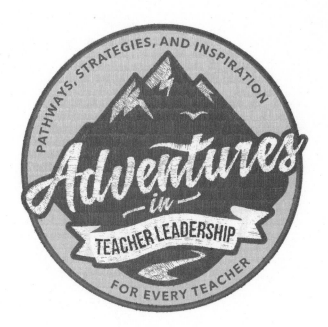

Adventures in
TEACHER LEADERSHIP

PATHWAYS, STRATEGIES, AND INSPIRATION FOR EVERY TEACHER

ASCD MEMBER BOOK

Many ASCD members received this book as a
member benefit upon its initial release.

Learn more at: **www.ascd.org/memberbooks**

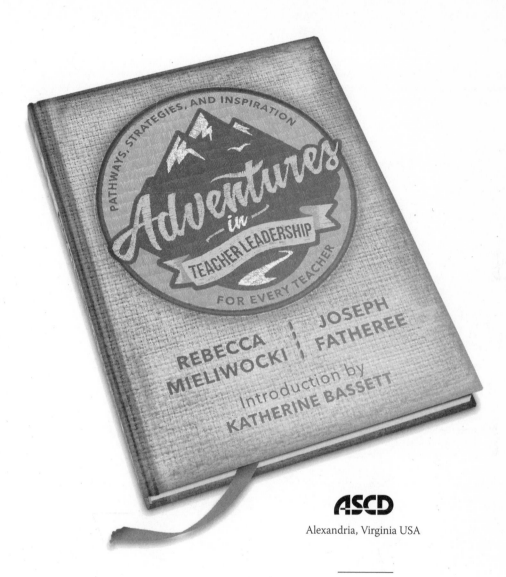

PATHWAYS, STRATEGIES, AND INSPIRATION

Adventures
in
TEACHER LEADERSHIP

FOR EVERY TEACHER

REBECCA
MIELIWOCKI | JOSEPH
FATHEREE

Introduction by
KATHERINE BASSETT

ASCD

Alexandria, Virginia USA

————

NNSTOY
TEACHERSLEADING

Philadelphia, Pennsylvania USA

1703 N. Beauregard St. • Alexandria, VA 22311-1714 USA
Phone: 800-933-2723 or 703-578-9600 • Fax: 703-575-5400
Website: www.ascd.org • E-mail: member@ascd.org
Author guidelines: www.ascd.org/write

614 S. 4th St. #335 • Philadelphia, PA 19147 USA
Website: www.nnstoy.org

Ronn Nozoe, *Interim CEO and Executive Director;* Stefani Roth, *Publisher;* Genny Ostertag, *Director, Content Acquisitions;* Susan Hills, *Acquisitions Editor;* Julie Houtz, *Director, Book Editing & Production;* Miriam Calderone, *Editor;* Judi Connelly, *Associate Art Director;* Georgia Park and Donald Ely, *Senior Graphic Designers;* Keith Demmons, *Production Designer;* Mike Kalyan, *Director, Production Services;* Trinay Blake, *E-Publishing Specialist;* Tristan Coffelt, *Senior Production Specialist*

All web links in this book are correct as of the publication date below but may have become inactive or otherwise modified since that time. If you notice a deactivated or changed link, please e-mail books@ascd.org with the words "Link Update" in the subject line. In your message, please specify the web link, the book title, and the page number on which the link appears.

PAPERBACK ISBN: 978-1-4166-2716-6   ASCD product #118033
PDF E-BOOK ISBN: 978-1-4166-2718-0; see Books in Print for other formats.
Quantity discounts are available: e-mail programteam@ascd.org or call 800-933-2723, ext. 5773, or 703-575-5773. For desk copies, go to www.ascd.org/deskcopy.

ASCD Member Book No. FY19-6B (Apr. 2019 PSI+). ASCD Member Books mail to Premium (P), Select (S), and Institutional Plus (I+) members on this schedule: Jan, PSI+; Feb, P; Apr, PSI+; May, P; Jul, PSI+; Aug, P; Sep, PSI+; Nov, PSI+; Dec, P. For current details on membership, see www.ascd.org/membership.

Library of Congress Cataloging-in-Publication Data

Names: Mieliwocki, Rebecca, author. | Fatheree, Joseph, author. | Bassett, Katherine.
Title: Adventures in teacher leadership : pathways, strategies, and inspiration for every teacher / Rebecca Mieliwocki, Joseph Fatheree, and Katherine Bassett.
Description: Alexandria, Virginia : ASCD, 2019. | Includes bibliographical references and index.
Identifiers: LCCN 2018053254 (print) | LCCN 2018059369 (ebook) | ISBN 9781416627180 (PDF) | ISBN 9781416627166 (pbk.)
Subjects: LCSH: Teachers--Professional relationships. | Educational leadership.
Classification: LCC LB1775 (ebook) | LCC LB1775 .M545 2019 (print) | DDC 370.71/1--dc23
LC record available at https://lccn.loc.gov/2018053254

27 26 25 24 23 22 21 20 19   1 2 3 4 5 6 7 8 9 10 11 12

All across the United States work the tireless and happy teachers I adore. They are determined and unstoppable, passionate and purposeful. Their hearts and minds are open for all learners as they pour every ounce of themselves into their work. Miraculously, each day spent educating their kids fills them right back up again. For every teacher who dreams big for kids, for every teacher who wants more for his or her school, for every teacher who takes up the cause of our profession and advocates for us—this book is for you.

—Rebecca Mieliwocki

———————

This book was written for those teachers past, present, and future who have suffered and sacrificed beyond human measure to ensure all children have hope for a better tomorrow.
You are my heroes.

—Joseph Fatheree

———————

For the researchers who gave us a foundation for teacher leadership; for the teachers leading before teacher leadership was even a term; for all those who have stood boldly to serve and forge new roles as teacher leaders, making schools learning communities for all students—you have my gratitude.

—Katherine Bassett

———————

Preface

I must be crazy, right? There's no other explanation.

When I began teaching in 1995, I was that nutty teacher who not only loved the performance aspect of teaching but also was hyped about lesson planning, paper grading—even faculty meetings. I shopped at teacher supply stores on the weekends and spent Sundays doing and redoing bulletin boards. I would find colleagues in the hallways at break times to chat about students and seek advice. I would grab my principal for walk-and-talks when I saw her heading somewhere on campus. I signed up for every committee, extra duty, or task force that was offered. I traveled to conferences on weekends and in the summer to learn from teachers who were smarter than I. Thankfully, no one ever told me to give it a rest already, even though they would have been justified in doing so. I was over the top, but I think there must have been something about my enthusiasm and sheer glee that kept my obsessions from becoming too annoying.

This passion for all things teaching and learning crept into everything I worked on and thought about while I was at school. I would sit at my desk, long after the kids had gone, and wonder, *Could I partner with my colleagues for cross-curricular projects this semester? Could our faculty meetings be more productive and empowering? How can our school partner with businesses to bring experts on campus to teach kids?* It was a relentless series of naïve musings that kept me hustling to make my teaching and my students' experiences better every year. I wanted so badly to make school a vibrant and wonderful place for my colleagues to be. Thankfully, I had an amazing principal who believed in me and who said yes far more than she ever said no and a husband who is my absolute rock and who supports every kooky teaching dream I manage to have. Because of them, I was able to do some remarkable things for teachers and kids that still have me floating on air. At the heart of everything I've done is a pure, unrepentant love for kids and for the adults who teach them.

In 2012, I was named my school's teacher of the year. Nominated by colleagues, I was honored and humbled to be selected as an exemplar of excellence in teaching by the people I myself looked up to. The process of being a teacher of the year required me to complete an application for my county's competition and then my state's. That application process was a crash course in U.S. education practices and policies that opened my eyes to all the good—and some of the not-so-good—that is our professional landscape. I wrote about it all, and my ideas about how to make it better, with all my heart and soul.

To my utter shock and disbelief, I made it all the way to the final rounds and was named both California Teacher of the Year *and* U.S. National Teacher of the Year for 2012. (The State Teacher of the Year and National Teacher of the Year programs were created in 1952 to recognize the contributions teachers make to society. Recipients of the title serve as advocates for the teaching profession during their year of recognition.) You could have knocked me over with a feather when I found myself standing next to President Barack Obama in the White House receiving the crystal apple on national television. How on Earth could I have won such an honor for just being my super-nerdy self and doing the work I loved so much that I would do it for free? (Shhh, don't tell my bosses!)

It turns out I wasn't crazy at all. I was a teacher leader, only I didn't know it because our profession never offered that role as an option.

When you are a State Teacher of the Year, you are thrust into an arena with the other amazing educators who have been given the same recognition by their states. Suddenly you realize the awesome enormity of what teachers are doing in classrooms across the country. You find your teacher twins (lots of them, actually) and learn that they are working exactly as hard as you are, doing all the crazy things you've been doing, halfway across the country or in the state right next to yours. The experience is beyond inspiring and just a little bit intimidating, but in a way that makes you want to work ever harder and be even better.

Spending time with fellow educators who cared like I cared and weren't shy about it showed me how much we have in common. I learned that at the heart of each one of these teachers was more than a love for kids or for their craft; there was a fire that burned hot. This fire compelled them to do more, to learn more, to change what needed to be changed, and to constantly work to make things better in education. Each of us had unique talents and passions that pushed us in different directions; but even in the differences, I saw so many skills and practices in common being employed in the work.

The funny part was that none of us came to this work through any traditional pathway or program. No university or teacher training program had forged us into leaders. We'd made our way on our own, just doing the next right thing as it came to us and benefitting along the way from a lot of hope, opportunity, and chance. If that was the case, was the teacher-leader journey destined to be a haphazard process forever? That possibility worried me.

I wondered if these skills could be catalogued and shared in such a way that any aspiring teacher leaders could read about them, recognize them, and begin to use them to chart their own leadership journey. Thus an idea was born. The book you are reading is the playbook for any teacher who ever wanted to be more of a leader but wasn't sure how to get started. It's for teachers who have had success with their initial leadership forays and are ready to take the next big steps.

Why a book? Because not everyone knows what teacher leadership is. I sure as heck didn't. It is an amorphous, undefined thing, and there is no compendium of examples for interested teachers to look to or follow. There isn't even a clear picture of who the nation's teacher leaders are. We know there are phenomenal teachers spread across the country, but what are their names? What do they do differently that makes them great, makes them leaders? For the first time, this book attempts to illuminate who teacher leaders are, what they do, how they do it, and how you can follow their lead in creating great change in your own educational sphere.

—Rebecca Mieliwocki

Rebecca's journey into teacher leadership is dramatically different from mine. Talk about success! I was named department head my very first day as a teacher. That may sound impressive; however, the truth is I was the only teacher in my department. I taught at a very small rural school in central Illinois, with only 15 students in the graduating class. My classroom was in the basement next to the boiler room. I felt isolated and alone the first time I stepped into that classroom back in the fall of 1989. The school struggled financially, so there were not a lot of resources available for a new teacher fresh out of college to use to help create engaging lessons. The Internet had not yet come to life, so I did the next best thing: I talked to everybody. I searched the countryside for teachers and community members who had developed interesting lessons or knew how to tell engaging stories. I had spent my undergraduate years trying to learn the *science* of teaching; I quickly realized that, as a first-year teacher, that was not going to be enough. If I really wanted to reach students and take them places they had never dreamed of going, I had to immerse myself in the *art* of teaching.

My work that first year was not good. I had a lot to learn, so I searched for mentors. Unfortunately, they were few and far between. I moved to a new district the following year and took a position teaching English to at-risk students. The community was very progressive and filled with entrepreneurial thinkers. However, the school followed the same traditional model that so many others around the nation continue to use today. Leadership was reserved for the administration. Teachers followed suit by going back to their rooms, closing the door, and teaching their students. That process may have worked well for others, but it didn't for me.

My principal said I was the school's first "basic English specialist." I was proud of that fact—until I learned what it meant. The school administration had decided to move away from dividing up the challenge of teaching the group of students who needed the most attention and resources and give that task to the lowest person on the totem pole. That was me. The majority of my students absolutely hated school. Attendance and discipline were major issues, and grades didn't matter to them. Most of these students had struggled for so long that the significance of receiving another low mark failed to register. I soon discovered that the practical problems I faced on a daily basis as an early-career educator were vastly different from the theoretical ones we had debated in college. I tossed most of what I had learned in college in the trash and started from scratch. It was an extremely frustrating time in my life. As a result, given the complete lack of support, I understand why so many early-career educators consider leaving the profession.

However, what I soon discovered was that my students were a great group of kids who struggled with self-confidence. Sure, there were academic issues that needed to be addressed. However, the biggest challenge lay in trying to help them believe in themselves. A few months into my new job, one of them said, "Mr. Fatheree, I don't know why you are trying so hard. We go from dummy math to dummy science to dummy English, and frankly you're an idiot for thinking you can teach us anything." Dumbfounded, I walked away from that day looking for answers.

My teacher leadership was born out of necessity. I decided to either figure something out or find a new career. Let me tell you, there wasn't a line of people standing at my door waiting to help. It was either sink or swim. I decided to swim.

Thirty years ago I started a quest to find people who could guide me in the right direction. I started asking them to serve as my mentors. Things started to improve. At first, it was hard and really embarrassing. I felt humiliated to have to ask for assistance. However, I quickly learned how wrong I was to feel that way. The world was filled with people who really cared and wanted to help. Since that time, I have built a vast network of resources. One of my goals has been to find as many ways as possible to share that information with other teachers. That's one of the reasons I am so excited to share the information in this book. My hope is that it becomes a valuable tool in your toolkit for success. We need educators like you who are willing to advocate for the profession. If we don't, who will?

Rebecca and I both share a great love of teaching. We want this book to be a guide for any teacher who feels that same fire inside. We know you; we know who you are; we *are* you. We know you are unique and that you have interests and strengths that are yours alone. But maybe you've been spending a lot of time wondering what more you might do, or who else you might partner with, or how to jump into the national conversation around educators. We hope that this book, designed around five key leadership avenues and packed with strategies to use, pitfalls to avoid, and teacher leaders' stories—including our own—will illuminate a pathway for you to travel on and will give you good advice along the way.

Teacher leadership isn't for everyone, but it *is* for lots of us, and we need all the help we can get along the way. Let this book be your guide as you choose your own leadership adventure.

—Joe Fatheree

Introduction
Katherine Bassett

I began my work in the field of teacher leadership in 2007, when I was asked by my then employer, Educational Testing Service, to explore what a potential career continuum for teachers might look like. Working with a 35-member consortium of stakeholders, I led the development of the Teacher Leader Model Standards (Teacher Leader Exploratory Consortium, 2011), a foundational document that outlines seven domains of teacher leadership. The standards were released in 2011 and are used by more than 20 countries in addition to the United States.

Katzenmeyer and Moller (2001) refer to "awakening the sleeping giant" of teacher leadership in their book of the same title as they talk about helping teachers to develop as leaders. And the "sleeping giant" metaphor was apparent in 2011, when I would talk about teacher leadership and get a lot of blank stares in response. What is teacher leadership? Where can we see it in action? Why do we need it? These are questions I frequently heard when talking about teacher leadership.

This situation has changed. Why? I believe that there are three key reasons. The first is that we are facing a serious issue of retention of both teachers and principals. The work of Susan Moore Johnson and her colleagues (2005) with beginning teachers, of Richard Ingersoll (2003) with career teachers, and of Ellen Behrstock and Matthew Clifford (2009) with

Gen Y teachers tells us that teachers are hungry for leadership roles beyond the walls of their own classrooms; not finding those roles and facing a dearth of opportunity to have an impact on decision making that affects their work, they choose to leave the profession.

A second reason the situation has changed is that the role of the principal has become increasingly difficult. Charlotte Danielson (2009) says that the scope of the principal's role makes the necessary work impossible to accomplish. And when we think about what we have done, layering multiple observations of every staff member onto an already full workload, we can see that the task truly is impossible. Without modeling of distributed leadership, which is not typically taught in principal-training programs and does not often exist in schools, principals have no one to go to in order to distribute leadership tasks.

Finally, there is growing recognition that the very culture of this thing we call "school" must change. We work within an egalitarian culture, in which no one teacher is supposed to "rise above" or purport to have attained expertise in the craft of teaching. How can we have a profession without experts?

In 1980, Dreyfus and Dreyfus presented a five-stage career continuum of growth leading to expertise that can be applied to virtually any profession (with some modifications of stages). Although this model has its critics, its fundamental message—that expertise is acquired in stages, is gained on the job, and results in expert practitioners—has merit. But in teaching, the only continuum that we typically have consists of leaving the classroom and going into administration. And when we do create roles for teachers that allow them to demonstrate expertise—such as coaching or mentoring—teacher leaders often encounter what Dediu (2015) and others refer to as the "tall poppy syndrome," being ostracized or criticized by peers. Fortunately, this situation is now beginning to be recognized as a problem and, with training, can change.

Mark Smylie (1992) talks about the need for training of teacher leaders. What he calls the "anoint and appoint" model of teacher leadership simply does not work. Just as we had to learn to become awesome teachers, so too must we learn skills to serve as teacher leaders. The skills inherent in working with adult learners are key to successful teacher leadership, for example.

The National Network of State Teachers of the Year (NNSTOY), in partnership with American Institutes for Research and other organizations, conducted a three-part research study looking at what exemplary teachers tell us about teacher leadership. These studies, *From Good to Great* (Behrstock-Sherratt, Bassett, Olson, & Jacques, 2014), *Great to Influential* (Jacques, Weber, Bosso, Olson, & Bassett, 2016), and *Investing in What It Takes to Move from Good to Great* (Jacques, Behrstock-Sherratt, Parker, & Bassett, 2017), contain important lessons regarding teacher leadership. They include the following:

- Teacher leaders have and model a growth mindset that promotes continuous improvement and innovation.
- Teacher leaders promote collaboration and self-reflection through roles such as mentoring, which can build more intentional and effective teaching practices.
- Teacher leaders connect research and practice as adjunct professors, guest lecturers, cooperating teachers, and mentors.
- Teacher leaders help beginning teachers translate effective practices to their own teaching style through modeling. Likewise, formal recognition may make teacher leaders more willing to model practices for others.
- Teacher leaders may feel more comfortable taking instructional risks and promote a culture of continuous improvement.
- Distributed-leadership structures and supportive school leaders can help facilitate teacher leadership roles and grow teacher leaders.
- Both formal and informal teacher leadership roles can support teacher leadership.

These findings are important as they come directly from State and National Teachers of the Year and finalists for State Teacher of the Year, many of whom serve, or have tried to serve, as teacher leaders in a variety of settings.

This book is important. It focuses on specific examples of teacher leaders at work, sharing their successes and challenges, and telling their stories about how they managed to find their place as leaders and contribute to student and school success. They learned important lessons along the way and share those with all of us.

In order for teacher leadership—and our efforts to retain great teachers and principals in our profession—to succeed, we must learn from these expert educators, apply the lessons that they have learned, and take important next steps to change our culture. Doing so will enable teacher leadership to thrive and a true career continuum, allowing for expertise, to exist.

1

Building Bridges: Using Communication Channels to Strengthen Ties, Create Networks, and Sustain Relationships

The art of communication is the language of leadership.

—James Humes

At Northstar Elementary School in Salt Lake City, Utah, the 5th grade classroom of Mohsen Ghaffari, Utah's 2015 State Teacher of the Year, is filled with kids from all over the world, many of whom do not speak English as their first language. As a matter of fact, over 22 different languages are spoken by the students at Northstar. Although they may not share a common tongue, Mohsen's students all come from families in which both parents care deeply about their child's success but must work incredibly hard just to survive. It is difficult for these parents to have the time and ability to participate in school life. Because he could identify with this exact situation as a result of his own schooling in Tehran, Iran, Mohsen knew that the best pathway to success for his students would require him to build a bridge that brought parents much closer to the school.

Meanwhile, in the remote rural town of Holderness, New Hampshire, Angie Miller's 6th grade language arts students faced significant challenges owing to their isolation and lack of access to the wider world. Angie knew her students might not be able to travel throughout the world, but they could certainly study about it in her class in meaningful and relevant ways. Angie's curricular invitation to explore this wider world was a powerful motivator for kids who might be born, grow up, live, and die in the same small patch of New Hampshire. New Hampshire's 2010 State Teacher of the Year, Angie knew that her students needed a connection to something bigger that could only be achieved if she found a way to unite teachers in a common purpose.

Across the country, Paul Anderson, Montana State Teacher of the Year for 2011, struggled to figure out how to maintain relationships with the students in his fast-paced advanced placement classes. His AP science classes required him to plow through vast quantities of information in an effective way while also providing his high school students with lab experiences in which they could conduct plenty of hands-on experiments. With only a limited amount of time to do many important things, Paul became painfully aware that many of his students needed more of his time, attention, and help than he was able to give during class. He realized that if he really wanted to work individually with groups of students, he could no longer stand in front of the class and be in charge of everything. He had to create a structure that allowed students to engage in learning on their own before they came to his class.

The situations each of these teachers faced relate in some way to communication, and they are not uncommon. After all, every teacher struggles with communication on some level. Rebecca was no exception. When she began teaching, she had some pretty clear ideas about what the job would be like. She'd plan and teach fabulous lessons, work with small groups and individual kids, and assign and grade student work. She'd keep a great-looking classroom, interact positively with her colleagues, and contribute to her school's culture. Sounds easy, right?

Pretty quickly it dawned on her: what she *thought* it would be like was not the same as what it really *was* like. Rebecca learned, as we all do, that the job of teaching is much more demanding than we ever thought it would be. Every new year and each new crop of kids brought a dozen unique wrinkles that needed to be ironed out in order for Rebecca to feel as though she was making an impact. Staying on top of all of these demands took every shred of intellect, enthusiasm, and energy she had.

After teaching for a few years, Rebecca began to notice some problems in the system that were preventing her and her school from being the very best they could be. Informal conversations with teaching colleagues helped her see that these problems weren't unique. They focused primarily around communication issues and the troubles that come when schools and teachers aren't communicating very well. Here's what she discovered.

Too many schools can be islands unto themselves, castles of learning whose drawbridges are pulled up, leaving families, teachers, and administrators disconnected. Families sometimes don't receive inviting human contact from schools, leaving them unsure about what's happening inside the schoolhouse and uncertain about how to help their children succeed. Parents and community partners, a potentially powerful and wonderful resource for schools, go untapped.

Things often aren't much better inside. Teachers become isolated from one another and are so fully consumed with the work of teaching that communication is hurried, infrequent, or task-driven. When they do have precious time together, it is typically reserved for administrative minutiae or so overly micromanaged that they are left uninspired, disconnected, and unheard.

Rebecca realized that opportunities for meaningful collaboration among colleagues were stymied by communication channels that weren't available, weren't open, or didn't fulfill the needs of the teachers doing the real work. Limited time and sheer exhaustion were keeping even the most committed teachers from reaching out to find others to share ideas and inspiration with.

In our own classrooms, there's often more material to teach than there are days in the calendar. Finding a balance that allows for meaningful practice, discussion, and work is a Herculean task. We don't always know how to get all the work done effectively and still have time to make deep connections with our learners.

Passionate and committed teachers—and we count ourselves among them—already know that each of these realities presents a huge hurdle to overcome. But here's what's important: rock star teachers are never content to sit back and let the status quo rule. No way! The best, most determined of us will turn ourselves inside out to knock down the walls that keep us from communicating clearly and well with one another. We will create a free and empowering exchange of ideas where once there was none. We will roam the halls of our schools to find kindred, collaborative spirits. We will reach out to our parents and our neighborhood community to make key connections. We just will. Why? Because we know that excellent communication skills can help us smooth and resolve a good chunk of the challenging situations that confront us. Such skills can even help us lay the foundation for exciting learning experiences for our students, their families, and our colleagues.

Strategies for Supercharging Your Communication Skills

We might not always be quite sure what to do, but as teacher leaders, we figure out how to make the tools we *do* have work to solve the problems in front of us. In the following sections, we take a look at some essential skills you can employ on your campus—or anywhere in your work life—to supercharge communication and guarantee success.

Let Down the Drawbridge

Do whatever it takes to throw open the doors of your classroom and your school for anyone and everyone to come inside. Increasing the communication flow between all the folks who make up a child's academic and home life pays enormous dividends. Matthew Kraft and Shaun Dougherty (2013), researchers at the Harvard Graduate School of Education, illuminated the impact of communication in their 2012 study, which found that increased levels of school-to-home communication resulted in a whole host of positive benefits, such as increases in student motivation, academic engagement, homework completion rates, appropriate classroom behavior, and stronger student-teacher relationships.

These results tell us that step one in an effort to improve communication is to publicize the fact that your school and your classroom are always open to visitors; that colleagues, parents, administrators, and community members are welcome; and that you will do whatever it takes to get the good word out about what's happening in your class. Opening your doors and your work to others lets in a wonderful bit of sunlight that demystifies and strengthens the school.

Take Your Class Online

In today's world, teachers who maintain a digital presence in the form of a teacher or a class website have a leg up on those who don't. Most schools and districts have websites with live links to teacher and class websites. If your school's website software comes with free teacher pages that you can use, go for it. If not, there are dozens of free programs like Weebly or Squarespace or WordPress that offer attractive, easy-to-use templates to create a website of your own. Although some teachers create sites full of impressive features, you can start more simply. Include your name and contact information, descriptions of curricula and materials for your classes, a calendar listing important events, homework uploads or links, a wish list of things you'd like to have donated, and opportunities for parent or community involvement. If you like, you can include your gradebook, pictures of student work products, or a tweet stream if your class has a Twitter account. You can even include a class mascot who posts a word, a fact, a math problem, or a quote of the day. At its core, your website is the place where families and students can gather to get essential information about your class and to connect with you.

Translate Everything

Roughly half of the classrooms in the United States have students who speak a language other than English (Quintero & Hansen, 2017). In some schools, dozens of languages are spoken by the students and their families. It is crucial to make sure that families are not left behind because important information about your class is not available in a language they can understand. Making this accommodation may seem like a simple thing to do, but the process of getting everything translated can take time. Early on, find out who on your campus or in your district is responsible for translation services. Make sure that you get your "welcome back" letter, your syllabus, your class guidelines, all major assignments, and any paperwork related to end-of-year events translated into the languages spoken by the kids in your classroom. You can use Google Translate or other translation apps to help with on-the-spot translations for e-mails home, and you can even add Google Translate to your teacher website so that parents can view it in their first language with a simple click of a button.

Activate the Parent Network

Most schools welcome parents on campus only twice a year, at back-to-school night and open house. Arts or athletics events might bring some parents to campus more often. These occasions provide a great starting point, but the best teachers invite parents to class a lot more often.

At least twice a year, invite parents to come to school to participate in the learning your students are doing. For example, you can host a parent science night with some sort of forensic "mystery" to be solved, a coffee-house event featuring kids performing poetry and music, or a "math madness" night with families competing against each other on math challenges. Next, you might ask parents to come in during the day to help you facilitate learning stations or to act as community experts and share their work or other expertise with students. If you want to go all in, survey your parents to find out where their passions lie and then figure out how to capitalize on that information by having them guest-teach a class, arrange a field trip, or facilitate a larger learning opportunity for your kids. Parents are an enormous, largely untapped resource, but teacher leaders know that there's gold in the parent community.

Mohsen Ghaffari, the teacher we introduced at the start of this chapter, knew this fact very well, and he decided to take relationships with families beyond back-to-school night by celebrating his culture through a home-cooked meal:

> I began by deciding to cook some food in my classroom and invite all my students' parents to come enjoy it with me. While they were there, I would share with them the latest research into child development and learning that they could use to understand their children better. We sent home

invitations, translated into many of the 22 different languages spoken at North Star, and I waited for the crowds to arrive.

His effort got off to a slow start, but in time, the payoff was well worth it:

> My first parent night was, how shall I say, lightly attended. With the help of translators, sign language, gestures, and a lot of smiles and laughter, I told parents where their children were developmentally. I explained what an 11-year-old brain can do that a 10-year-old brain cannot. I spoke about my expectations for their [children's] work, and ways they can help their sons and daughters excel, not just at school and at home, but in life too. This was the imperfect but wonderful beginning of many times I invited families to be part of what was happening in my room.
>
> What I realized was that even though they say a teacher is where the rubber hits the road, there are many, many parts to the machine that make this car go. I might be the wheel, but if everyone doesn't know what to do or how important they are, the car cannot move very well. Parents must be brought into the circle so they can feel they are a part of their child's success.

Provide Weekly Updates

Whether via your teacher website, a folder sent home, or a routine e-mail blast, provide parents and families with a weekly update letting them know the academic focus for the coming week, what concepts will be covered, what tests or quizzes are planned, what extra help is available, important schoolwide events for the week, and anything else you want parents to know about. You can even include a family "challenge question" that they can take part in. For example, we've seen teachers send home fun "Where in the world is this?" geography questions, quick-write topics about family traditions, or even lists of the world's most difficult-to-spell words. For some reason, kids just *love* giving their parents quizzes. Trust us.

Here's why the weekly update is so helpful. Teachers are often bombarded by parent e-mails, and finding the time to answer them all in a timely way can be tough. Often the e-mails contain questions about the items just mentioned. Sending out a proactive update each week answers dozens of questions that families now won't need to ask via e-mail. The regular update also gives them a feeling of confidence that they will be able to help their child navigate that week's learning and work successfully.

Talk with Parents in a Respectful, Positive Manner

In any situation where you are talking to parents, make it a priority to demonstrate a deep respect for them, their time, their child, and the situation at hand, no matter what it may be. Parents see you as an expert education professional. It's important to wear that mantle in a calm, positive, confident way. Aim for every interaction to be a win-win scenario that leaves all parties feeling that something good has been accomplished. When something great has happened in class, dash off a postcard, an e-mail, or a quick phone message. Let parents know what great thing their child did and why you are proud. Do this at least once per week, if not daily. Parents *love* positive news from school. This gesture puts a lot of metaphorical money in the bank for times when you need help or when the news from school might not be so great.

When a tough conversation is in order, use positive presuppositions before approaching the difficult or hard-to-hear part of the conversation. For example, if you have to make a call home about classroom misbehavior, you could begin by saying, "I know it's important to you that your daughter behaves well in class; it's important to me, too. I also value and appreciate your input because I know you are the expert in things relating to her. I am calling today to get some support for some things that are happening in class lately." Laying this groundwork indicates that you (1) respect the parent's role and knowledge, (2) are assuming good outcomes in advance, and (3) are willing to work together to solve problems. Parents have often had so many less-than-wonderful phone calls from school that they tend to prepare themselves for the other shoe to drop as soon as you introduce yourself. Beginning the conversation as just described disarms them and helps them see that you are approaching them from a mindset that isn't angry or accusatory, but instead curious and in need of assistance. Most parents want to help and are happy to be asked to provide suggestions, solutions, and feedback about how to make things better. If you can get and keep parents on your side, there's almost nothing they won't do to help you.

Keep Your Door Open and the Welcome Mat Out

Traditional school structures often find teachers siloed into their class-room spaces and scheduled in such a way that deep, meaningful, and stimu-lating interaction with colleagues is tough. It takes a concerted effort to fight this structure, but it's absolutely worth the expenditure of your time and energy. The first thing to do is to make sure everyone you work with knows your door is always open, and that for better or for worse, you welcome any-one to pop in to visit anytime. You might even press them into service or ask them to participate in what the class is learning.

Take care with this step and how you deliver your welcome, as it's a fine line between being genuinely interested in having visitors and coming off as the know-it-all teacher who wants everyone to come see your amazing instruction. You want to approach this as someone who is curious about getting better and aware that one of the best ways to do that is to have colleagues come see you teach. Next, ask your colleagues who *do* come by to give you feedback on what they saw. Whether it's via a quick sticky-note reaction or some advice about a targeted moment of the lesson, make it clear that people who come can't leave without reflecting on what they saw. You can even ask your administrator if your school can start a pineapple chart or an #ObserveMe rotation—two ways to encourage informal observations or instructional rounds at your school. (Visit https://robertkaplinsky.com/whats-difference-observeme-pineapple-charts for a simple description of these approaches.) This is how we get better—by seeing, and being seen by, our colleagues.

Bring Colleagues Together

However possible, find other teachers on your campus to collaborate with. You can start on a small scale by finding one other teacher with whom you feel a positive connection, or you can reach out to all of the other grade-level teachers on your campus. You could go bold and ask the entire faculty to join together around an idea you can teach all students. It doesn't matter what you do, only that you do it. Why? Because there's a lot of research out there about the array of benefits that teacher collaboration has on students. Tami Burton's 2015 study, *Exploring the Impact of Teacher Collaboration on Teacher Learning and Development*, says teachers who actively engage in collaboration report a greater range of skills. Pounder (1998) and Smylie, Lazarus, and Brownlee-Conyers (1996) found that teacher autonomy negatively influenced student achievement, whereas team accountability positively influenced it. John Hattie's (2001) groundbreaking research reported in *Visible Learning for Teachers* positions collective teacher efficacy as the number one factor influencing student achievement. When teachers work together, everyone wins. So think about who on your campus might be willing to work with you on a lesson, a project, or an activity that will benefit your students, and ask if that person will join forces with you. If the answer is no, don't take it personally. Keep trying. Eventually you'll find someone who's as happy and excited to team up as you are.

Look for Connection Points

Once you've found some willing collaborators, it's time to meet and plan. This step takes strong organizational and interpersonal skills. First, decide together on the best time to meet, and then set aside this time and guard it. Don't let anything but essential interferences (like a parent conference or a personal emergency) keep you from getting together. Once together, keep the meeting as informal in tone and energy as possible to put everyone at ease, but ask someone to be an unofficial facilitator. By doing so, you can make sure that your time together is efficiently managed and effective and that you accomplish what you set out to do. Every time you meet, set a goal for the meeting, keep time, and do your best to be productive. At the end, take stock of where you're at and what the next steps are for everyone. Follow up with an e-mail to the meeting participants with a recap and the agreed-upon next steps.

At the first meeting, decide what kind of projects or ideas you'd like to try. Here there are no limits to what you might do. You could dip into the shallow end and do a "lesson swap"—you borrow a lesson from your partner and your partner takes one from you. You both teach the lesson, collect artifacts from students, and get back together to discuss how it went. You could plan complementary lessons with a teacher who teaches a different subject. Once, when Rebecca's class was reading "Zebra" by Chaim Potok, a short story about a Vietnam veteran who is an amputee, she collaborated with her science partner, who spent two class periods on the topics of phantom limb syndrome, amputations, and prosthetic technology. The students' knowledge and sense of engagement skyrocketed. Rebecca and her colleague couldn't wait to find more places to sync up.

You also could jump into the deep end together and dream up large projects that affect a whole grade level. Many schools have Old World Fairs, Unity Days, or Harlem Renaissances that involve every teacher teaching a lesson or series of lessons on the art, music, politics, and literature of an era, along with related lessons in science and math, and students working together to create products they show off on a designated day. The key is to find out where your standards, curriculum, and content overlap with those of other teachers. Once you know that, it's time to dream. Think about ways students could have their learning made more exciting. Are there current events that lend themselves to a collaboration? Is there something big you've always wanted to do, like a Gatsby Day, but needed help from other teachers to pull off? Are there ways to bring math, social studies, English, and science—along with art, music, and movement—into one set of lessons that ignite your students and their passion for learning, perhaps through something such as an Olympiad or an Innovation Day? The answer is yes. You and your collaborators just need to uncover those ways.

This kind of situation is what lit Angie Miller's teacher fire. She knew her sheltered students needed to know the world beyond New Hampshire, but she also knew this was a job best suited to all of their teachers, not just one. Here's how she explains her effort:

> I began small, by creating units for my middle school classroom that focused on areas of the world facing crisis. Students would study about Pakistan, Haiti, or natural disasters that had happened around the world. First, my

students would read everything we could get our hands on about the subject. Then they would invite experts or government officials to visit our classroom to share what they knew, and my students could ask questions about how to get involved. After reading and hearing from outside experts, we would work together to form a plan to help. Often my kids would organize and host fundraisers in the community to raise money to help those who were affected by the crisis we'd learned about.

After several years of working on projects like this, I began to feel that itch—the itch we all have when we're ready to grow. I wanted to see if there were like-minded people on my campus who could partner with me to make the kinds of projects my students had been doing even better.

This is how it begins for so many of us—that feeling of wanting more for our students than we can create on our own, an urge to remove the walls of our classrooms to reach out to others who also aspire to bigger experiences. Angie took the initiative and found those folks who would be willing to go on a journey with her:

In our first year, a group of teachers who shared the same students partnered to create an integrated unit of instruction on Sudan. The humanitarian and political crisis in this East African nation was everywhere in the news, and students already had a general understanding that something devastating was happening that needed more attention. The collaboration spanned all six of the teachers the students had each day. In my English class, students were reading about Sudan. The science teacher was teaching students about the geography of Sudan, natural resources, and the desertification of the terrain. The social studies teacher was discussing the political climate and crisis there along with the history of the nation, while the math teacher worked on population and life-span projections. The music and art teachers were major contributors to helping students see, learn about, and make East African art and music, and the students' computer teacher taught students how to house their work for the entire unit in digital portfolios. It was astounding to see how natural a fit it was to combine our talent and expertise to help widen the world for our students.

Meet People Where They Are

When you enter any relationship in which you want collaboration and authentic connection, it's imperative that you meet people where they are most comfortable. Some teachers collaborate all the time and are no stranger to linking arms with a compatriot to plan a project. They understand and are excited by the collegial give and take—and sometimes the messy truths—of this kind of work. They know how to manage the work flow, the grading, the parents. And they seem to have a kind of courage about opening up their practice and their classrooms to curious others. These teachers tend naturally to take the lead in planning and pushing the team; this is their gift. It's important, if you're that person, that you temper your own passion and enthusiasm—not because those are bad qualities, but because sometimes this level of energy can feel like a steamroller coming so hard and fast that it can scare people away.

Others may never have worked closely with another teacher—ever, on anything. By choice or circumstance, there are a great many lone wolves out there. These teachers need kind and gentle coaxing to join into the collaborative space where ideas and planning are shared. They need verbal and nonverbal reassurances that joining forces creates a kind of synergy we struggle to create on our own. Once they feel connected, protected, and part of the team, they're in.

Finally, it's important to realize that each teacher's comfort level with collaboration is different. Some want to go all in and trade kids, rotate through stations, build an entire day around a project with parent volunteers and a community outreach piece. Other teachers would run screaming at the thought of a project of this size and scope and instead favor sharing a common text to analyze, or starting an activity in their class that a colleague finishes in his. Whatever feels right to all members of a collaboration unit is OK. Just try to build successes, for yourself and for students, that you can continually build upon. Teachers are like kids. They need to see something working well, and often, in order to buy into it all the way.

All of us have high standards that we expect our students to meet. When it comes to teacher collaboration, it's OK to have those same high standards.

But standing above the fray and expecting teachers to magically reach them on their own doesn't work. You've got to watch, listen, and take time to understand exactly where people are so that you can take their hand and go forward together. Doing so requires being a master communicator.

Attend to the Unspoken

Teaching is such a busy business. So much happens between 8 a.m. and 3 p.m. that interactions between teachers, administrators, staff, and even parents are often more hurried and less efficient than we wish. It's easy to get wrapped up in the frenetic swirl of getting things done, but true and deeply satisfying communication happens when we attend to the nonverbal needs of the humans we work with.

You've probably met someone who does this and remembered your interaction with him or her long after the moment was gone. That's the hallmark of a strong interpersonal and nonverbal communicator. These people pay extra attention to you. They make great eye contact. They smile more than most. They offer a gentle touch or an embrace when they see it will be received well. These teachers take time to check in with colleagues by asking after children, spouses, and other work or passions they may be pursuing. They match the postures and voice levels of those they are in conversation with. Great communicators are great listeners and observers of the human condition. When you attend to those qualities that make human contact satisfying, you find that people gravitate toward you and are happy to be led by you as well.

Be Teachable

Most teachers are experts and extremely knowledgeable about kids, their craft, and their content areas. Chances are you've met teachers who lead with an "I know it all already" attitude. There's nothing they need to do differently or better than what they already do.

Teacher leaders roll differently, in our experience. We don't tend to communicate that attitude outwardly, even when we feel confident. If there's something we have in common, it's an earnest humility about our work and a tendency to shun credit, even when we deserve it. We can debate the merits of that humility, but the one thing that stands us in good stead is that teacher leaders remain eminently teachable. We know that every day is an opportunity to learn and grow in new ways. We can hold on to a core set of ideas that we know generates success for kids while simultaneously seeking out new, different, and better ideas from outside ourselves. We know we have plenty to offer others and will do so if asked, but we also know that it's just as powerful to listen, learn, and receive from others.

Stay open. Listen more than talk. Try new ways of working. Share successes, but also speak openly and honestly about your trials and struggles.

View Personalities as a Plus

If you've met a dozen teachers, you've likely experienced a dozen different personalities. That's what's so interesting about us: we're all different, but we have a lot in common too. We come to teaching because we love kids and because we believe we can make a difference in the world. Typically, teachers are a pretty passionate bunch. Hang out at any faculty meeting and within 10 minutes you'll have a pretty good sense of the group.

This pageant of personalities makes teachers interesting, but it also makes navigating among them a challenge when you collaborate. Our advice? Embrace it all. Inevitably, someone you are working with is too loud, too quiet, too opinionated, not opinionated enough, too weird, too—you get the point. That's OK. Let the extroverts be the outward face of your work; let the intellectuals do their heavy cognitive lifting; let the hyper-organizers keep you on track and focused; and let the activists help negotiate the trickier aspects of the work you're trying to do. Everyone has a role to play that will help the work succeed. Realizing what a wonderfully complex, delightfully flawed group teachers are makes it easier to look beyond quirks or tendencies that might normally turn you off.

Consider Radical Access

Today's world offers incredible opportunities to expand the ways teachers can reach their students, and students can come in contact with people and places far beyond the classroom walls. The traditional lecture is no longer the only vehicle for delivering content. Teacher leaders everywhere are knocking down the classroom walls by using technology to create new communication pathways for students.

The most common way to create such pathways is by flipping your classroom. Decide what course content you'll record or create that students can experience at home, or somewhere on campus, before coming to class. Once in class, you are free to host hands-on labs, activities, or simulations that help kids contextualize and practice what they've learned. Teachers who flip have reported increased test scores as well as improved student attitudes, with particular benefits for students in advanced placement classes and students with special needs (Goodwin & Miller, 2013). According to Baepler, Walker, and Driessen (2014), students' outcomes in a flipped classroom were significantly better than those in a conventional classroom or a control class, and students' perceptions of the learning environment were also improved. Linking your content to your online classroom or to YouTube allows you to customize the user interface to allow for student questions, e-mails, and even family access.

It's a brave new world out there, and teachers are using the available tools to create new learning spaces online and on campuses everywhere. One of those teachers is Paul Anderson, the Montana teacher we introduced earlier. Using the technology work flow just described, Paul was able to create a digital "second classroom" where his students could visit to gather knowledge and information to prime them for the live, in-class experiences to follow. Here's how he describes what he did:

> Initially, I saw the emergence of the flipped classroom movement around the country and decided to use videos as a tool to disseminate information to my students so that we could maximize our time together in class doing actual science. I had been teaching traditionally for 13 years before I made my first video for students to watch at home or at school before my classes began. I created a website, bozemanscience.com, where students could see

all the material related to my class, and that's where I uploaded videos for them. There was a "Contact Me" link on the page where kids in my own classes could start giving me feedback on the videos or make suggestions for improvement.

Between the website, the videos, and the curated resources for students like lecture notes, graphs and tables, and articles, my students were better prepared for lab work and deeper academic discussions in class. What most teachers who flip their classrooms will tell you is that pushing the material out to students this way allows them to consume the content at their own pace, to pause and consider material more deeply, or to jot down reflections, questions, or potential misconceptions in a safe space. While the communication channel is mostly one-way, teacher to student, somehow it ended up expanding my students' understanding. In class, there was a deepening of comprehension and a true wrestling with the science in a way I simply did not have the time for with the more traditional stand-and-deliver framework.

Take Advantage of the Digital Universe to Build New Communities and Networks

Previously, teachers' entire network of support, outreach, and development consisted of the teachers they worked with, the ones they met if they attended conferences off campus, and any books they took the time to read on their own. Boy, have times changed for the better! In the last decade, virtually every wall that separates teachers from one another and the information superhighway has come down. Today's teacher leaders tap into a variety of helpful apps, programs, tools, resources, experts, and professional learning communities they can get to quickly with a single touch. The average teacher may create a digital classroom community via EdModo, Google Classroom, or Class Dojo; spend time watching teaching videos online via the Teaching Channel, Edutopia, or Teaching Partners; or communicate with a world full of amazing educators via Twitter, Facebook, Snapchat, and Instagram to find support, inspiration, new ideas, and opportunities. Teacher leaders do all of this and understand how much better they are at their craft when they have a diverse array of circles within which to communicate and grow.

Communication Pitfalls and How to Avoid Them

Sometimes it dawns on us how much of our productivity and forward momentum get stalled because of conversational quicksand. We've all left meetings where nothing was accomplished or had one-on-ones with colleagues that left us discouraged or angry because of communication mishaps. Here are a few tips to help keep you from sinking into that same sand.

Failing to Listen or Hear

In any conversation, make sure you are taking time to truly listen and hear what people are saying. Pause before speaking, and give yourself some time to think—just as you would do for your own students—before responding. Seek to understand what others are trying to tell you before you ask that they consider your viewpoint. These few small gestures communicate care and generate trust. They make people feel valued and respected. Rushing to respond, or using someone's talk time to construct your own response, tends to stymie efforts to reach understanding.

Being Defensive

Working together to make teaching and learning terrific is hard work. It involves honest conversation and, sometimes, direct and constructive criticism. Becoming defensive or hostile or mounting a counterattack will not help you solve the issue in front of you. Instead, take a breath. Recognize that you are experiencing something that might be painful but that it's important to stay calm. Realize that criticism is not a personal attack but an attempt to help you grow. If you feel brave enough, admit your discomfort with what's being talked about but affirm that you want to keep working on it. Take a break if necessary. Ask for time to gather your thoughts and then commit to reentering the conversation. When you do talk again, work toward a resolution in which both parties feel OK about what's been said. Being honest about your feelings and asking for time-outs help quell those feelings of anger or insecurity that can bubble up when teachers start to dissect their craft.

Being the Know-It-All

Some teachers make you feel you can learn and do anything. These teachers are connectors and builders of teacher efficacy. They reach out to others and welcome people into their orbits to learn and grow along with them. They aren't afraid to be vulnerable, to admit when they don't know the answer.

Then there are teachers who project a different aura. They tell you "it's easy" or "c'mon, everyone can do this" without seeming to comprehend that just because some instructional or professional moves are "easy" for them doesn't mean they're easy for everyone. These are the teachers who have an answer for every question and a solution for every problem. They've seen it all and done it all, and they like to tell you about it. After an interaction with a teacher like this, you often feel worse about yourself, not better.

Whenever possible—and it's always possible—be the first kind of teacher. Cultivate and communicate a presence that is wise, warm, accepting, and authentic.

Not Telling Your Story

When you withhold important information about your classroom, your students, or your school, you allow the narrative to be crafted by someone else. Nature abhors a vacuum, so where there is no information, some will soon appear—and you might not like what you hear.

It's essential that the people who work at your school be the authors of its narrative. Make sure that narrative celebrates all of the wonderful people and things happening at your campus. Be the champion your school deserves and shout from the rooftops, through every channel available to you, what's happening.

Lessons Learned by—and from—Mohsen, Angie, and Paul

In the scenarios at the beginning of this chapter, Mohsen, Angie, and Paul each wanted to create new networks that could allow them to work differently or better so their students could thrive. Creating these networks required new ways of communicating, on and off campus, with colleagues and with parents, during the school day and after. Here's what's worth noting about the three of them: when interviewed, each of them admitted they didn't know exactly what to do, only that they had to do something to break out of the circumstances they were in. That's a unique and common trait among teacher leaders. They don't let perfect be the enemy of good. Looking back at their stories, we can see how great successes can come from stumbling, tentative starts.

Mohsen began to see positive reactions to his sustained efforts. Over time, parents began asking him when he was going to invite them to school again. At the start of each year, those who had heard about his parent nights asked if he was going to host them again. Word was beginning to spread, and more and more parents looked forward to these invitations. But the enthusiasm wasn't just with parents; it spread among colleagues as well. Here's how Mohsen describes it:

> I decided to expand my outreach to include my colleagues and even [others outside] the walls of our school. Any time I went to a conference or learned something new about child development or brain research, I shared the information with my colleagues. I even decided to have an enormous poster made that hangs in our school lobby, so that every family entering the school had to pass by it. It's an infographic that tells of the impact, over a lifetime, that even a few minutes of reading can have on a child's brain and overall success. I had the information in the poster translated into Spanish and English, side by side. My hope is that by sharing the latest information about learning, all parents will better understand how to support their children.

Through the experience, Mohsen learned about listening and understanding the personalities you're working with. As he explains,

> You will be more successful if you know who your audience is, what they want for their children, and how to help them achieve their goals. There is much we may want to accomplish in our classrooms, but we must begin by respecting our audience and using our skills to bring them closer to the children and the work we do.

Mohsen also learned about the value of persistence and a willingness to stumble through an imperfect beginning. He emphasized that though the first step is the hardest, it does pay off, especially as more people engage with your effort to create the shift you need:

> You become a community of caring partners, bigger and more meaningful than you could have imagined. It takes a while and it's easy to get discouraged. Don't. Even if you reach one or two more parents than you had before, you've changed lives forever. It's completely worth it.

He also learned about how important it is to not move ahead alone:

> If there's something you care deeply about and you know it's good for all kids, find a way to spread the good news. Invite partners. Share what you have, and offer yourself as a resource for others when and if the time is right. Ask others to join you so that together, you can go far.

In New Hampshire, Angie discovered that she wasn't a lone wolf, and by taking the leap and asking around, she found an entire cadre of colleagues willing to open their plan books, their classrooms, and their students' potential by collaborating. She'll tell you it wasn't always easy—not by a long shot; but the things we're most proud of ultimately are the hardest to accomplish. She admits,

> [The] first year of working together was so rough. Different personalities and teaching styles caused some of us to butt heads or hit rough patches. I am a natural steamroller, and even though my colleagues knew this, and maybe loved this about me, it did create difficulties occasionally. We had never worked this closely together, so we were all learning how to do this the right way. However, the impact this work had on our students was undeniable, and we could see it. They were changed children. They were aware of a global crisis in such a clear, wise, and compassionate way that we couldn't help but be inspired by what they had learned and how they had grown.

The work was tough. It required that Angie monitor not only *what* she and her colleagues were doing, but also *how* they were doing it. In order for the students to experience a synchronized series of learning experiences, everyone needed to be in sync, and that required Angie to know how to build a team, keep lines of communication open, establish expectations that were reasonable and fair for all members, and make sure that everyone felt they were an equal part of the process. As she recalls,

> After the year ended, I knew that some of us might have wanted to give this level of constant communication, coordination, and collaboration a break; but our students excitedly pressured us the following year by asking what we had planned for them next. We had to admit that this ragtag tribe of connected teachers had done something wonderful that needed repeating. And so we did.

Angie's experience in communicating with colleagues leads her to provide two pieces of advice that need to be heard by teachers early in their careers and often after that:

> First, don't be afraid to ask for help. There are hundreds of smart, dedicated folks doing the work we are doing, and many are just waiting for a chance to be part of something bigger. We can't do everything we wish to do all by ourselves. So reach out. Ask when you need something; listen to advice from others; bring as many people as you can to whatever mission you have so that its success is guaranteed.
>
> Second, be honest and don't be afraid to be vulnerable. So often teachers are intimidated when we see great things going on in other classrooms, other schools, or in teacher leadership projects. We get overwhelmed with worry or a feeling of inadequacy because we are watching their highlight reels and we never see their struggle. We tend to overvalue their successes while undervaluing our own efforts. As you move into a space where you're working with other teachers, don't be afraid to share your stumbles and your successes. They give others the courage to begin the work themselves.

In Montana, Paul was originally looking for a way to get through his curriculum more effectively than he was able to do on his own. However, the experience of creating digital content for his students also created an entirely new professional pathway for him to explore, one that has taken him to nearly every continent on the planet. Here's his account:

> In 2000, I decided to post my first video to YouTube. It sounds [like a] cliché to say the rest is history, but it happens to be true in this case. There are now over 600 science videos of mine uploaded, which have garnered millions and millions of views—and not just by students. Teachers, school administrators, and school system leaders from nearly every continent and country have found my work to be incredibly helpful too. In many science classrooms, bozemanscience.com has become a familiar name.
>
> Putting my lessons out there allowed me to connect with students all over the world. What I started to realize was that I had two classrooms— [one composed of] the kids I dealt with daily and [the other composed of] all the people around the world who were seeing what I had put out there. After a while I realized it wasn't only students who were watching the videos but teachers were too. I began to receive comments, compliments, and shout-outs from the educators my videos were helping. Suddenly I was connected to a community of people all committed to teaching and learning about science. It was incredibly empowering, and this fueled my passion to do more and more.

Paul's first efforts were, by his own admission, wobbly; but like Mohsen and Angie, he didn't let that deter him. His process of trial, error, and success mirrored the scientific process he had spent so much of his life sharing with students. He's clear that the mistakes along the way made him better:

> I knew that I needed to keep learning and be willing to grow. I couldn't let being perfect be the enemy of [being] good enough. I spent hours and hours making and remaking my first videos, cutting out flubs and mistakes as I went. I thought, "Man, if they take this long, I'll never make more than a few." Instead, I began rolling the camera and just letting things happen naturally. If I had a flub or if I misspoke, I just calmly corrected myself and

moved on. My students loved seeing my mistakes, and it gave them something to tease me about. Teachers appreciated the genuineness of my unpolished videos. Eventually, [the videos] got quite a lot better, but don't be afraid to be imperfect. It helps more than you might think.

Paul's work has enlarged his professional sphere of influence enormously. Now, as a result of his teaching videos, website, and outreach to kids and teachers, Paul is in great demand as a teacher consultant helping districts plan and implement the Next Generation Science Standards and adopt excellent teaching practices in science. Initially Paul set out to be a teacher of kids, but his ability to connect and clearly explore the exciting issues inherent in his AP science curriculum means he's become a teacher to the world. Ironically, this role has him learning more and more each day, just like his students. As he says,

When you begin to lead, you realize that each day is its own master class. Be prepared to remain in a perpetual state of learning, perseverance, and growth. Even though it is exhausting and scary at times, it's also thrilling. I don't know all the answers, and I still need to do a great deal of work to be ready for what each day throws at me; but I relish the challenge. You will too.

All Aboard: Using Collaboration and Critical Friendships to Empower Everyone

I can do things you cannot, you can do things I cannot; together
we can do great things.

—Mother Teresa

Terry Kaldhusdal, the 2007 Wisconsin State Teacher of the Year, taught in a silo for the first 20 years of his career. During that time, he worked to develop a space where teachers actively sought out their peers to share ideas and ask for assistance. Terry knew the best teaching took place when teachers worked together to address the needs of their students. The camaraderie created a common bond that enabled the team to move mountains. However, progress was slow and at times frustrating. The doors of their classrooms remained closed. Little collaboration took place. Terry thought everything would change for the better when the decision was made to build a school within a school. However, the concept of placing a team of content specialists in a giant room with 120 6th and 7th graders and asking them to work together with no training created an entirely new set of challenges. Terry and his peers were forced to develop their leadership skills to survive. What would they do?

In another part of the United States, the concern of Ashley Lamb-Sinclair, the 2016 Kentucky State Teacher of the Year, increased as she watched the list of teachers' responsibilities grow while their time to collaborate decreased. The recertification process for teacher licensure in her state was particularly disturbing. In her school, teachers spent hours of their own time developing lesson plans and searching the Internet for information. They used a variety of different software applications to build a crude system for sharing information. Ashley understood the process was one of the lowest forms of collaboration. She was also highly agitated to learn that none of that work could count toward the teachers' professional development requirements. Armed with only an idea, Ashley was determined to change the system.

Living in the middle of the Kansas plains, Dyane Smokorowski, the 2013 Kansas State Teacher of the Year, understood the importance of ensuring that the students in her building had the same access to energizing field trips exposing them to the arts, culture, and people that other students had access to in large metropolitan communities. Additionally, she was determined to develop new instructional methodologies that provided students with the ability to unlock their creative potential. Initially Dyane was concerned with only the students in her building. Little did she know her work would create a firestorm that connected students around the world in ways never before dreamed possible.

Terry, Ashley, and Dyane understand that teaching is a team sport. Today it takes every teacher and administrator at a school working together at peak efficiency to handle the challenges of educating the nation's youth. Unfortunately, most teachers are forced to work in archaic systems that lead from the top down and do little to promote collaboration. In addition, few teachers have been provided the training necessary to enable adults to work together effectively.

This lack of training became quickly evident to Joe 30 years ago, when he was just entering the workforce. Like many novice teachers fresh out of college, his eyes were filled with the illusion of staff meetings where colleagues collaborated with one another to develop engaging lessons. That vision was quickly replaced with the reality of an isolated work environment. Like the bulk of U.S. schools, his lacked a structure that promoted the free-flowing exchange of ideas and the opportunity for staff members to provide ongoing support for one another. Real collaboration, the kind that promotes professional growth, did not exist. Instead, the staff adopted the "law of tooth and nail." In that world, only the strong survived. Teachers viewed the pecking order of seniority as a rite of passage. No one rushed to offer advice or share tricks of the trade. Veteran teachers grew stagnant in their practice. A first-year teacher like Joe, who taught high-risk students, teetered on the brink of becoming a casualty himself. The standing assumption adopted by the staff was that those who could teach did, while those who couldn't handle the pressure left the classroom with their tails tucked between their legs. The old unspoken rule of "Earn your stripes; then we'll talk" quietly passed from one generation of teachers to the next. Joe quickly learned he was all alone, and it was up to him to find a way to survive.

Does Joe's story sound familiar? Unfortunately, we find it repeated in schools all across the nation. Many teachers work in isolation, a situation that is particularly challenging for those entering the profession. Researcher Richard Ingersoll (2012) writes in *Education Week*, "This is difficult for newcomers, who may be left to succeed or fail on their own." Indeed, many new teachers quickly decide the profession is not for them. According to a report prepared for the National Commission on Teaching and America's Future (2007), as many as 20 percent will leave the profession in the first three years. Veteran teachers are also at risk.

A drop in teacher retention rates has caught the attention of global leaders. In 2015, international delegates gathered in Alberta, Canada, at the International Summit on the Teaching Profession to discuss issues that affect the profession (Asia Society, 2015). Teacher efficacy was one of the major points of discussion. Today, policymakers are pressed to find a solution to address the largest teacher shortage in history. According to the UNESCO Institute for Statistics (2016), 69 million *new* teachers must be hired by 2030 to ensure that every child has a teacher.

Teachers will tell you that one of the ways to reverse the trend is through the transformation of the stagnant culture that exists in most schools.

Teachers want to be valued and their voices heard. In the traditional top-down approach that still exists in most schools, teachers are told how, what, when, where, and why to teach. The vast majority of them spend most of their time in their classrooms with little opportunity to work together. This situation has to end. Teachers want to be involved in the decision-making process. They have a lot to share. We need a *collaboration revolution.*

Going back to Joe's experience as a new teacher and fast-forwarding 30 years, we find that things are dramatically different in his world. His district hired a new superintendent who understood the value of distributed leadership and the need for teachers to come together to create a culture that ensures students are prepared to take their rightful place on the global stage. But how do you reverse a ship that has been pointed in the same direction for decades? Joe's superintendent broke tradition and turned to him. The question is, why?

Determined to make a difference, Joe had built a massive network, over the course of 30 years, of renowned teacher leaders and educational advocates. Initially, he began the work to ensure that the needs of his students were met. However, he quickly noticed that other teachers he came in contact with struggled with the same issues. Through their collaboration, Joe and his associates around the country started a movement to empower teachers with the skills they needed to become leaders. His district finally took notice in 2016, when he was invited to Dubai to attend the Global Education Skills Forum and was named a Top 10 Finalist for the Global Teacher Prize awarded by the Varkey Foundation. Since that time, Joe has been asked to work with district administrators to create a training program that will provide all teachers and administrators in the district with the skills they need to collaborate with one another and develop critical friendships along the way. Their groundbreaking work is creating a new chain of command that has everyone talking with everyone else. The idea is to create a seedbed that promotes student and teacher innovation, where teacher collaboration fuels instructional creativity. The culture incubates ideas from teacher to teacher and from teacher to administrator, with the goal of transforming practice and policy at the building and district levels and, ultimately, positively affecting student learning.

One of the reasons teacher leadership has been slow to grow is a lack of examples. Stories like Joe's are few in number, making it difficult for administrators and teachers to know what the end result might look like and where they need to start. However, the business world is filled with examples of systems that value collaboration. Pixar is a great place to start.

In his book *Creativity, Inc.*, Ed Catmull (2014), president of Pixar and Disney Animation Studios, outlines the processes his team used to build one of the most creative studios in the history of animation. He describes a place where everyone is encouraged to talk to everyone else, where rigid chains of command no longer exist but are replaced with protocols that promote the free sharing of ideas; where teams of critical friends work together to solve complex issues; where failure is no longer avoided but is instead embraced as part of the learning process. Imagine what it would be like to work in a school that adopted those same principles and the value of teaching in such a place. Imagine department meetings filled with vibrant discussions that consider and respect all points of view. Imagine teachers feeling free to meet with one another outside team meetings to continue conversations without the fear of reprisal from their peers, learning how to have discussions that enable them to address difficult issues or ponder alternative points of view. Imagine individuals working together to craft a common vision that includes ensuring every student under their care develops the skills needed to succeed in life after graduation.

Inspired by examples like that of the creative world of Pixar, Joe and other teacher leaders are in the process of creating similar cultures in their schools to promote innovation. You can too.

Strategies for Increasing Collaboration and Creating Critical Friendships

As you begin your collaboration journey, don't worry about missed opportunities in the past or be afraid of what lies ahead. Your willing spirit can be the spark that ignites a leadership fire in your district. The following strategies are essential for developing a culture that supports collaboration among its members.

Build Trust by Breaking Down Walls

Trust is the foundation for all collaboration. It's hard to earn and easy to burn. Real trust begins with the ability to have ongoing conversations with your peers and show genuine interest in their stories. That's difficult to do if you stay within the confines of your classroom. It's time to break down the walls and start building relationships with your fellow teachers. What may seem uncomfortable at first will pay big dividends down the road.

Terry Kaldhusdal learned the importance of trust the day his district decided to literally tear down the walls in part of his school to build an instructional environment for a program called "Create." A team of teachers was asked to take on the challenge of collectively teaching over 100 students in a school-within-a-school concept. Here's how Terry describes the experience:

> The last two years, we have literally opened the walls of our classrooms. The destruction of those barriers exposed everyone in our group. It made me a better teacher and helped me learn how to use different techniques to reach kids. Over time, we have built trust in one another. That has helped take our teaching to another level. However, we discovered our growth had little to do with the absence of physical walls. It was all about the philosophy of developing a team that trusted one another to the point that complete transparency became the rule rather than the exception.

Building trust requires being honest with one another. Make sure to keep confidential any information that a colleague shares with you in private. Avoid joining in gripe sessions, especially those aimed at belittling another staff member. It's difficult to build a trusting environment if people are concerned about what you or someone else may say about them when they walk out the door.

Don't Underestimate the Power of One

Teacher leaders are typically born out of necessity. Most didn't seek the role; it found them. When a need arose, they took charge. Teachers are now leading department meetings, developing new curriculum, creating and presenting professional development sessions, and engaging in a wide array of other activities. Unfortunately, the vast majority of teacher leaders receive their training from the school of hard knocks. It's easy to understand why so many of them struggle with self-confidence. The numerous bumps and bruises that come from that style of learning can lead to self-doubt. However, it's important to remember during those times that leadership starts with one. Never doubt the transformative power that a single idea can have if it is birthed in the mind of a motivated person.

Ashley Lamb-Sinclair realized that the opportunity for the teachers in her school to participate in meaningful collaboration was severally limited. Frustrated, Ashley came up with the idea of developing an online platform and an app that enable teachers to share resources and engage in conversations to develop better lessons (see curiolearning.com). It is important to understand that she had no prior experience in developing software. What she had was a hunger to improve the collaboration and professional development processes for staff members. She saw that many teachers were using Twitter and Facebook as tools to access high-quality professional development instead of attending conferences. Unfortunately, in most schools, training delivered via those vehicles fails to count toward the continuous professional development units that teachers have to earn to maintain their license. Ashley struggled to understand the lack of vision: "That's the problem. We are working our tails off as teachers, constantly Googling and sharing with our peers. All this, then we have to hit the pause button and jump through some hoops for the powers-that-be just to get our credits." She was convinced there had to be a better way. Then Ashley had her "aha!" moment, and Curio Learning was born.

Ashley wanted to develop an online tool that provided teachers with the ability to curate, create, and share work they were already doing but in a more systematic way:

For example, my professional learning community at school uses Dropbox for teachers to store and share artifacts. Unfortunately, that's where the collaboration stops. Most teachers just download the artifacts and use them the next day. That's not real collaboration. Real collaboration is messy. It starts with an idea. You've got to talk through it before a decision is made as to how you are going to use it.

The app and platform are organized through stacks and cards. For example, two teachers decide to collaborate on a unit for *Romeo and Juliet*. The teachers work on their own time to search the Internet for resources, which they store and share on digital cards. Groups of cards are stored in stacks. The teachers can collaborate with one another by leaving comments or questions on the cards. The cards serve as living documents that a teacher can copy and edit to personalize a lesson. The original owner of the card is given credit for creating the lesson. As Ashley explained, "Almost everything online [is] already premade or prepackaged. I don't know too many good teachers who print it off and teach as is. There's no real collaboration in that." In other words, Ashley's vision of creating an online space for teachers to share and collaborate started with the same best practice that she used daily at her school.

Most teachers will not follow Ashley's path and develop a new software package. However, millions of teachers use an array of social networking tools and software packages to connect with one another every day, often resulting in limited collaboration. As a teacher leader, you can organize a team to identify your collaboration needs and find the appropriate tool for the task at hand. You can lead the effort to simplify the process and promote the sharing of information and the professional discourse that is necessary to develop amazing lessons and grow a collaborative environment outside the walls of your school. Ashley believes "you can never be too assertive when it comes to creating new opportunities for yourself or your students." Don't be afraid to pursue your dreams.

However, as a leader it is important to consider how you "wear" the role and the success that follows. Try replacing the word *I* with the word *we* as often as possible. Talk less about yourself. Praise the work of your teammates and find ways to validate their work. Provide opportunities for them to share their ideas without interruption. Remember to show empathy when things don't go as planned. Your teammates will be much more forgiving as you develop your leadership legs if you remember to show a little grace along the way.

Remember That Failure Can Lead to Learning

Failure is one of the most misused and overlooked tools in education. It is something we teachers are encouraged to avoid at all costs. The problem with that approach is that failure is unavoidable. It is an inherent part of the learning process. Don't miss out on an opportunity for you and your team to grow as professionals by constantly trying to avoid failure and running away from it. You can either collapse under the weight of trying to escape failure or thrive by learning how to deal with it.

The first step is to accept the fact that everyone fails. Own your failures and don't beat yourself up over them. Even the best fail. Famed inventor and entrepreneur Thomas Edison once said, "I've not failed. I've just found 10,000 ways that won't work." He understood that failure is part of discovery. Take time in your team meetings to discuss why something isn't working. Be slow to place blame. Instead, focus your energy on dissecting problems and brainstorming solutions. The air becomes less toxic when you work as a team to solve problems.

Next, don't look at a failure as the end of the road. Your success as a teacher leader will be gauged in part by your ability to navigate barriers. The question is, do you see possibility where others find a dead end? The explorer Thor Heyerdahl once said, "Borders? I have never seen one. But I have heard they exist in the minds of some people." Researcher Carol Dweck (2008) calls that attitude a growth mindset. Discuss as a team what your corporate mindset is on issues that stymie growth and stop your group from moving forward. Are you fixated on what you can't do, or are you looking for solutions to address the issues that you have some control over? Terry Kaldhusdal's team understands the value of modeling for one another—and for their students—how to handle failure. "We have an attitude of learning by doing. I've always asked my students to embrace their failures, learn from their mistakes, and the teachers in my school are living that belief."

Obviously some situations are more difficult than others, and more planning is required to address them. In those instances, consider meeting as a team to do a SWOT analysis (an analysis of relevant strengths, weaknesses, opportunities, and threats). The ability to connect with your peers to conduct such an analysis is the first step toward the development of a strategic plan. Don't forget to include a list of names of critical friends who can help you overcome challenges.

Stop, Look, and Listen

Teaching is exhausting. Even the best of us can be worn down by the juggling act of planning and delivering multiple lessons to diverse groups of students, running from meeting to meeting, and trying to stay ahead of the paperwork. One of the last things teachers usually have time for at the end of grade-level or department meetings is reflection. But not making the time is a mistake.

Create a space where your team has quality time for reflection, and make it a sacred part of your culture. Make it the one place where you can stop and look at where you have traveled, and where you can laugh and cry together. And make it the place where you can collectively dream about the future, make plans based on lessons learned from past mistakes, and build on success.

Terry's team understands the value of reflection. According to Terry, "The entire team now schedules a meeting once every two weeks where we comb over student data. This forces us to take time to reflect on everything from our practice to our schedule. These reflections help us determine what's working and what needs work."

Set the mood by bringing snacks, playing light music, or gathering in a location that promotes collegiality. Be honest with one another and ask the hard questions. The ability to have courageous conversations is a byproduct of an environment built on trust. It's important to address issues when they surface instead of letting them fester. Listen to your teammates and respect their views. Help everyone remember that you're all in this together. Don't let anyone rob you of this experience. It provides you with an opportunity to develop a common vision, which is a vital first step—and one that many overlook—in building a powerful collaborative team. Don't gloss over the importance of doing this work. The final product will be the compass that helps guide your team through rough patches on the route to success.

Recognize Celebration as the Great Driver of Success

Even more difficult for teachers than finding the time to reflect is having the ability to celebrate success. One of the first things teachers learn is to keep their successes to themselves to avoid professional jealousy, which runs rampant in many schools and is a major issue that needs to be addressed. Used correctly, celebration can be a powerful motivator to drive positive change in schools and beyond. The inability of teachers to share their personal journeys and the incredible work that takes place in their classrooms is one of the most powerful reasons that people outside the system develop negative feelings about education. All they ever hear is the bad news that comes out of schools. The good is rarely discussed.

If you really want your team to grow, consider how you can take on this challenge. Discuss during your team meetings how you can help celebrate the success of your peers. At the same time, be aware that celebrating the success of others may open up feelings of self-doubt in some people. Instead of lifting others up, some will tend to focus on what's wrong with themselves. Remind one another that wherever someone is on the teacher leadership journey is OK.

Celebrations can range from the grand to the extremely simple. Here's Terry's description of one way his school celebrates success:

> Two years ago my principal brought in a great idea that my colleagues still revere. Before each staff meeting he asks if there are any "rock stars" among us. At that time a staff member will celebrate a colleague and present a painted rock. Laughs are often part of the presentations, and sometime there

are even heartfelt tears. Staff members across the building proudly display their rock on their desk. It's simple, it's cartoonish, and it's fun; but best of all it helps build an environment of trust, understanding, and success.

Find a way to celebrate everyone's work at some point, but be careful not to make the process resemble an award ceremony for kindergarten soccer, where everyone gets a trophy. Instead, discuss how you can lift up your colleagues in meaningful ways. Surprise notes, cookies, or just sharing how honored you are to work with your peers will transform your culture in ways you never dreamed possible. Discuss how you can share good news in the media and with parents to let the greater community know about the positive things that occur in your school. Also, don't shy away from having an occasional conversation with one another about how your team should wear success. For example, saying thank you and carrying yourselves with humility help ensure you're sharing accomplishments and accolades in the appropriate manner.

Collaboration Pitfalls and How to Avoid Them

Effective collaboration may look seamless and simple to do, but don't fall into the trap of believing the development of a robust culture comes without effort. Here are a few simple steps to guide you.

Failing to Establish Norms

The best way to guarantee a dysfunctional team meeting that no one wants to attend is to avoid establishing norms. In today's fast-paced society, every second counts. People don't have time to waste at meaningless meetings where little is accomplished.

Do your team a favor and work together to establish the norms or rules that everyone will be expected to abide by during meetings. This simple step can bring order to your meetings and make them something people want to attend. To get buy-in, make sure that everyone in your group is present on the day the norms are established and that everyone gets to share their thoughts on the topic.

Consider who will be in charge of running the meeting. Will that role fall on one person or will it be shared? What will the chair's responsibilities be? Make sure to outline those responsibilities to avoid confusion. Establish a common date and time to meet, and hold to it, so that everyone knows how to plan around the meeting schedule.

Consider creating an agenda for each meeting. Agendas provide order and ensure the right topics are in line for discussion. Develop a process for creating the agenda, making sure that all stakeholders have a chance to add to the list. Distribute the agenda before the meeting so everyone comes prepared. During the meeting, stick to the agenda. Create a "parking lot" for ideas that come up during the meeting but are not among the items scheduled for discussion. Circle back to them if there is time at the end or move them to the next meeting. Respect everyone's time by starting and ending meetings on time.

As a team, make it a regular practice to revisit your norms. Doing so helps everyone to remember how important it is to abide by them. Dyane Smokorowski describes why norms are an important part of creating a robust learning environment:

> Norms are established at the first face-to-face meetings, and they are never a set checklist of items. I believe handing out a set of norms in a meeting is similar to going over the syllabus on the first day of class—[it's] painful and doesn't open any doors to relationships.
>
> My workshops are never a sit-and-get format. Instead, teachers are up and moving, collaborating, giggling, and learning by doing. Periodically throughout the workshop, I will pause, talk about an activity that was active and involved discussion, and then share [that] these are the norms I expect—active voices, active bodies, and positive culture. Additionally, for activities where teachers are expected to collaborate, I provide sentence stem starters to help conversations get going.

Staying in Your Silo

Teachers in many schools remain in their siloes throughout the day, rarely if ever visiting their colleagues' classrooms, inviting others into their classrooms, or gathering with peers for collaborative efforts. This kind of professional isolation limits any opportunities for the professional growth that comes from sharing knowledge and experience for the common good.

If you want to break free from the grip of the status quo, the best way to start your collaboration journey is to walk out of your classroom and into that of one of your peers. But before you do so (they'll wonder why you're there!), take time during a team meeting to discuss the benefits of visiting one another's classrooms. Develop a protocol that will provide your team-mates with the opportunity to learn from one another. Terry describes the importance of those classroom visits:

> One of the things I missed when I was in my silo was the ability to watch others teach. I had that experience during my practicum. Once I started teaching, the opportunity was gone. I couldn't walk into another classroom during my prep period. If I did, people would ask what I was doing. They wanted to know what I wanted. The last two years, we have literally opened the walls of our classrooms. The destruction of those barriers exposed everyone in our group. It made me a better teacher and helped me learn how to use different techniques to reach kids. Over time, we have built trust in one another. That has helped take our teaching to another level.

Terry's experience is rare. Most teachers will never have the opportunity, as he does, to teach in a customized instructional space that is designed to hold hundreds of people. However, that doesn't mean you can't benefit in the same way he did. Talk with your peers and administrators about how to build this kind of "open" experience into your work day. Also, don't forget to discuss what you want to learn and how to do so in a way that is nonjudg-mental of your peers. Classroom visits are intended to be an observation tool—not an evaluation—to improve one another's teaching practices.

Trying to Become an Expert in Everything

A troubling issue in public education today is the idea that teachers have to be masters of everything. An unrealistic expectation, to say the least, this notion will only lead to frustration and resentment.

Do your best to confront the "masters of everything" mindset with a more reasonable alternative that highlights the strengths of your team members. Conduct a strength analysis to identify each member's unique gifts, and use the results to help distribute the workload. Likewise, work together to ensure that one person is not carrying an unnecessary amount of the load. Use the SWOT analysis you conducted earlier to identify the characteristics of critical friends who might be outside your immediate network and discuss ways to connect with them.

Living in rural Kansas, Dyane understood the importance of connecting her students and staff to experts outside the community, as illustrated by this example. Determined to find a renowned authority to help her students better understand digital piracy, Dyane turned to Skype. After scanning the Internet for someone who might talk with her students, she unearthed the name of the CEO of the Motion Picture Association of America. After repeated phone calls, she eventually was able to talk to him. Skype was new at the time, and he had no idea what the program was; but he agreed to schedule a call with her students. As Dyane describes it, "That day my students came to school dressed up to talk with this amazing human. During the call, you could [almost] hear the 'ahas' . . . in the minds of my students. Magic happened. That experience changed the way I would teach moving forward." Dyane came to see Skype as a way to build an incredible network of critical friends that would help students and teachers collaborate like never before. She was asked to help start the Skype Master Teacher program that helps connect teachers around the globe. The lesson here is this: think outside the box and consider using one of the many social media tools that will enable your team to expand its connections exponentially.

Focusing on the Negative Instead of the Positive

Negative talk is one of the best ways to create a toxic environment that stops collaboration in its tracks. Why not reverse the trend and work together to focus on the positive attributes of your school?

Switching from negative to positive may appear easier than it actually is. Negativity is everywhere, and schools are far from immune. Don't believe it?

At your next team meeting, work with your peers to generate a list of issues and concerns that are plaguing your school. It won't be long until page after page is filled with complaints. Then ask your peers to generate a second list, of positive things happening at your school. Compare the two lists when you are finished, and think about what has been shared.

Focus on the negative list first. Ask yourself, are the items complaints or issues? There is a difference; both are important. Complaints are typically problems that we just need to get off our chest. Everyone needs the occasional chance to vent about something that is bothering them, and it is important to provide a safe place for those conversations to take place. Usually a quick rant is all it takes. People generally feel a lot better after they've released the emotion and can move ahead. However, some complaints linger, and the owner struggles to let them go. Left unchecked, constant complaints can destroy the culture you're working so hard to create. At some point, a courageous conversation is in order to help your peer move on. Talk about how to do this in team meetings and agree to hold one another accountable.

Likewise, there are real issues that people struggle with. They tend not to be easily fixed, and it's best to work as a team to help one another overcome such problems. One of the first steps is to think like a researcher and contextualize the problem. Can you boil it down to a single sentence? If so, work together to find out why it is a problem and what the possible solutions are. Teachers tend to get frustrated when administrators don't help them with their problems. Ask your team if you have articulated the problem well enough to your administrator so that person can discern whether it is a complaint or a real issue. Consider whether the administrator must operate under limitations that make it difficult or impossible to provide assistance. For example, it's difficult for administrators to help if they are only allowed to talk with certain people and share only fractions of a particular story. Most administrators don't have the time to play cloak-and-dagger games to solve the "he said/she said" dramas that contaminate the cultures of many schools. Work with your team to address these kinds of issues before they become a problem. At the same time, don't be afraid to approach your administrator with real issues. However, be willing to share the work you and your team

did to come up with possible solutions. Most administrators like problem solvers. They will also appreciate that your team knows the difference
between a complaint and a real issue and that you valued their time by trying
to address the situation before coming to them.

Move on to the list of positive items once you've reviewed and dealt with
the negative list. Don't skip this step just because the list is not filled with
problems. Some may see this as a waste of time that could be better spent
putting out fires, but keep in mind that you can't put out fires if you haven't
taken the time to build a fire station and train the firefighters. Take time out
to discuss all the items on the list and how those points have affected student
learning and the staff. Celebrate the victories and discuss how you can work
together to create a culture where the focus on good far outweighs the focus
on the bad. As a team, try to spend more time focusing on the positive. The
more you work at it, the easier it will become, and positivity has the power
to transform a building. Stakeholders come to quickly understand that you
and your team are willing to take on tough issues but refuse to let bumps in
the road contaminate your outlook. Cultures like this are desirable places
to teach. The work may be hard at times, but the positive outlook helps to
create a fun, safe place where people feel comfortable being themselves.

Sometimes, you just need to laugh. No one understands that more than
Dyane. She works hard to keep the mood light and positive energy flowing in
the right direction:

> I purposely keep a YouTube playlist of improvisational comedy or silly pet
> videos in my favorites. Even five minutes of giggling can help bring balance
> to a situation and allow me to look at it with clarity. I think that might be
> why I thread improv games and activities into my workshops with teachers.
> Giggling is a positive stress reliever and helps to clear the mind before tack-
> ling the next challenge.

Becoming Paralyzed by Fear of the Unknown

For the most part, teachers are creatures of habit. In the past, teachers
focused on one thing: teaching the students in their classrooms. Like it or

not, things have changed. Today's schools are fast-paced systems that require all hands on deck. Teachers are required to collaborate with other adults on a daily basis to make informed decisions on the fly. That can be a scary proposition for teachers who have never been asked to share their opinions or lead a group. A few years ago, the decision-making process was pretty simple: come to work with a willing attitude and do what you are told, and everything will be OK. That's no longer the case. Schools in the 21st century are organic systems whose complex issues require a new level of expertise and collaboration with a vast array of individuals. The first step outside the door of your silo can be scary, but remember that there is strength in numbers. You have a great team; all they need is a leader. Leaders don't always have all the answers. What they do have is a can-do spirit that helps them take another step forward.

Teacher leaders accept the fact that the unknown will be a part of their day-to-day experience. They have confidence in their teammates and believe their team can take on any challenge that is set before them. Terry, Ashley, and Dyane had little training on how to work with their peers to create robust learning environments. However, they all believed that teaching can be more productive if people are willing to work together to develop a common vision.

Terry quickly saw the potential a collaborative environment could have in meeting the needs of his students. It also did not take him long to see how ill-prepared his colleagues were to handle such a change after his district approved a major renovation to create the school-within-a-school program. A construction crew was hired to knock down the dividing walls between a number of classrooms and build a giant instructional space. The teachers didn't think much about it at first. However, once they began teaching in the new space, it quickly became evident that their ability to collaborate and develop partnerships would be critical to the overall success of the program. Imagine placing a team of content specialists in a room with 120 6th and 7th graders and asking them to work together with no training. As Terry explains,

In a traditional classroom you have your kingdom in a silo and your desk. In the new space, all of the teacher desks were put into one room and placed along the wall in a U-shaped pattern. We didn't really think much about how the architect designed that portion of the space. However, we soon discovered it was a tight spot. The teachers were constantly on top of one another. I did more collaboration in that two weeks of school than [I had done in] my entire 20 years of teaching.

Another issue quickly surfaced. The group did not have a single leader. According to Terry,

It was democracy at its purest. Nearly every single decision was debated. You had six teachers with very different ideas as to what education should look like, what their education had been, and what their strengths were as teachers. One of the things we learned was the importance of taking the time to build community. Unfortunately, we did not take the time to build a mission statement or a philosophy. The group didn't discuss what personalized learning was. You can ask 10 different teachers and get the same number of answers as to what the world should look like. That caused a lot of friction. It was the toughest two years of teaching I ever had.

The journey was a fascinating evolution for the teachers. By the end of the second year, the team had grown to include two special education teachers, two literacy instructors, two math teachers, and a science teacher. Terry taught history. The program also added a class of 8th grade students. Through their journey, Terry's team discovered how to work together for a common goal. The teachers built in time for reflection and worked to ensure everyone's voice was heard. The project was so successful that the number of students who were interested in participating doubled. Terry was asked to lead the development of a second cohort.

Walls or no walls, Terry's determination to overcome the challenge of a system that promoted isolation—and to dismiss fear of the unknown by being part of an innovative program contained within a dramatically renovated instructional space—is a striking example of what is possible. As you consider Terry's example, think about how you can overcome fear of the unknown and promote collaboration among peers in your building.

Dyane is another example of a teacher leader exemplifying the benefits of overcoming fear of the unknown. Today she provides support to approximately 325 teachers in the Andover school district in Kansas. The teachers are divided into groups and participate in innovation academies for two years, during which Dyane helps them conduct deep-dive sessions into pedagogy and the development of innovative lessons. Dyane has worked diligently to develop an elaborate network of teacher leaders, critical friends, and businesses that span the length of Kansas and encircle the world. Programs like Skype Master Teacher have provided the teachers in her district with an unlimited knowledge bank of resources that they can use to help prepare their students for the global stage. Dyane and her colleagues continue to work together as a team to provide a world-class education for their students.

Never has it been more important for our students and staff to learn how to connect with diverse audiences across the globe using multiple forms of technology. The world is growing smaller by the day, while its issues are becoming more complex. One of the greatest gifts you can give your students is the ability to connect with people in other places. You and your students will be challenged by diverse perspectives and learn the true meaning of empathy. The digital space provides you with the ability to connect with people who live in some of the most remote regions of the Earth. However, the connectivity also comes with limitations. There will be issues along the way. Technology won't always work correctly. Language barriers or cultural differences may impede your progress. Still, the importance of creating cultural connectivity cannot be overstated. As a team, think about where you want your global journey to begin. Dip your toes in the water before diving in head first. Crowdsource a list of critical friends from your peers and start following them as a group. Consider asking a renowned authority on a topic to join your group via Skype for a brief discussion. Develop a growth plan that challenges your group to make this effort a priority.

Lessons Learned by—and from—Terry, Ashley, and Dyane

As illustrated by the strategies and anecdotes shared in this chapter, collaboration is one of the most powerful tools in your toolbox for success—although it takes practice. For the better part of his career, Terry longed to work in a collaborative environment where teachers freely shared ideas and worked together to create a learning space that inspired student creativity. However, once the opportunity presented itself to teach in such a space, he struggled.

Terry's woes are not unique. They were the result of a lack of training and understanding of just how limited true collaboration is in most school buildings across the country. Fortunately for Terry, he and his team had a can-do attitude that helped them overcome the struggles of working in a completely transparent environment that allowed everyone to see the best and worst in one another on a daily basis. They learned along the way how important it was to ensure everyone's voice was heard and to clearly define roles and responsibilities. The culture started to improve as time passed. Terry understood this was a once-in-a-lifetime opportunity, so he chose to take the high road and work with his teammates to develop a plan that would help them navigate the bumps in the road to make the program something special for their students.

Ashley's persistence in developing a long-term digital solution to assist teachers in their collaboration is noteworthy, but not because of the scope of her project; very few teachers would ever take on such a task, and that's OK. Ashley's story is important because she understood that a culture that supports strong collaboration does not happen overnight. The old adage that Rome was not built in a day holds true to her story—and yours. Spend time thinking about and discussing with your team what the return will be on your investment in collaboration. This is important because you are asking your teammates to invest a lot: you are asking them to allocate time, stretch their comfort zones, abandon past practices, and work with others to develop a new culture. These investments have the potential to profoundly transform your learning and teaching space. Ashley had a clear vision of the desired outcome and the perseverance to see it through. Do you?

Finally, Dyane's issue of isolation can hold true in classrooms in urban centers well beyond the plains of Kansas. She embraced the idea of using an approach that was nontraditional at the time to connect her students with the world. Today, many tools such as Skype are readily available for teachers to use, whether they plan to invite authorities to discuss a wide array of topics or connect with other teachers to discuss best practice.

The experiences of Terry, Ashley, and Dyane demonstrate that mastery comes through constant use and the willingness to self-critique and learn from others. By tearing down the walls of their siloes, these three educators helped incubate cultures that supported collaboration and student learning. The message is clear: don't be afraid to ask others for assistance; have the courage to take that next step. You never know where your collaboration journey will take you.

3

Travel Routes: Pathways for Creating Effective Professional Development

If you want to go fast, go alone. If you want to go far, go together.

—African proverb

Cameron McKinley, Alabama's 2007 State Teacher of the Year, hadn't taught very long before she noticed how much time and energy teachers were devoting to systems that could be easily streamlined—for example, by converting from a traditional grading system to an online grading system. Having enjoyed an exciting decade-long career as a marketing manager and systems engineer for both IBM and the United States Air Force Reserves, Cameron took her experience and a degree in corporate finance to the public schools. There she was inspired to use her skills to make a difference in the world by working with middle school kids. Using her enthusiasm and considerable tech know-how, she brought her school online with a digital grading system that brought relief to her hardworking colleagues while demonstrating a variety of unique uses for technology in the classroom. Cameron eventually got so busy helping her colleagues, she realized she couldn't both help teachers and teach her own classes very well. Something had to give.

Across the country in Burbank, California, Rebecca, a 7th grade English teacher and California's 2012 Teacher of the Year, was experiencing implementation fatigue. In her two decades of teaching, she and her colleagues had been exposed to, and were expected to master, over a hundred different programs, standards, pedagogies, strategies, curricula, federal policies, and technologies. Always flashy and filled with promise out of the gate, nearly every initiative her district adopted eventually either faltered or fizzled out entirely. It wasn't because teachers like her weren't trying their best to adopt and use them—just the opposite. Rebecca and her teacher peers never got enough systemic support to see any one thing launch properly and endure over the long haul. She made a promise to herself that if she was ever in a position to stem the tide of educational "silver bullets" foisted upon teachers, she would immediately take it on and instead reorient teachers around what *really* works to promote their growth: close collaboration with one another around the work they do with their kids.

In Baltimore, Maryland, Josh Parker, 2012 Maryland Teacher of the Year, was seeing firsthand the educational inequities that children of color face in the United States. Having taught secondary English for 16 years and seeing how low expectations were damaging poor kids and kids of color, something deep within propelled him to pursue the goal of guaranteeing that a complete and challenging standards-based literacy education would become a part of every child's experience at his school. But to do that would mean he'd need to take on more than just one classroom of children at a time. Now an instructional coach at Paul Lawrence Dunbar High School in Washington, D.C., and an English cohort leader for UnboundEd's Standards Institutes, Josh's passion for unlocking student potential comes into play as he works with teachers to undo some of their biases and unlearn the habits that have kept too many children from achieving the success they deserve.

The experiences of Cameron, Rebecca, and Josh represent different takes on one of the greatest ironies in all of teaching. Brand-new teachers are expected to be as effective on day one of their service as the veteran teacher working next door. Similarly, experienced teachers are expected to grow and improve over time through the professional development provided to them throughout their careers by their districts. The glaring reality is that (1) very few teacher-credential programs adequately prepare teachers for the complex set of challenges inherent in the work, making true readiness rare; and (2) very few professional development opportunities provide cohesive, meaningful, or enduring paths to excellence for teachers.

Let's face it, for a great majority of us, preservice preparation left much to be desired. Many of us report not being prepared for the realities of the profession upon entering the classroom. Most of the training we received and desperately needed as new teachers happened once we were already on the job. When shallow preparation is combined with uneven or nonexistent support for skill building, teacher development is left to luck and chance.

When it comes to inservice professional development, teachers suffer again. Districts may have unfocused visions for such development. Or maybe they expect teachers to participate in and pay for their own. Maybe they offer none at all. In far too many schools in the United States, money is allocated to train teachers in the next exciting program or pedagogy with little practical support, no coherent overall vision in which to situate the training, and no long-range analysis of its effectiveness relative to the effort and time devoted to it. Perhaps you've worked in a school that experimented with a professional learning community (PLC) model but left adequate training and guidance unattended, making true collaboration and goal-reaching haphazard or frustrating. It's no wonder most teachers roll their eyes at the mention of new professional development efforts each year. They are exhausted and frustrated as a result of repeated unsatisfactory, ineffective experiences. In short, the situation is a mess. How can we expect millions of teachers (National Center for Education Statistics, 2018) to improve steadily to keep pace with innovations in teaching and learning when the systems designed to do that work just *don't work*?

In a Learning Policy Institute survey of research on effective professional development, researchers Linda Darling-Hammond, Maria E. Hyler, and Madelyn Gardner (2017) analyzed 35 studies that demonstrated a positive connection between teacher development activities and outcomes for students. Their findings echo what so many of us know from our own experiences: the most effective growth practices for teachers are content-embedded, incorporate active learning, provide plenty of time and resources built into the workday for teacher collaboration, employ teacher leaders and expert mentors to drive the work, adhere to a cohesive set of best practices that an entire faculty engages in for more than a moment in time, and allow for feedback loops and personal reflection to power teacher learning and student achievement.

We know that the fastest path to improvement is a constant focus on the teaching craft led by teachers who understand the classroom, how kids and adults learn, and how to move the needle on achievement through continuous, focused, and challenging professional development experiences. Sometimes those challenging experiences look like individual mentoring or instructional coaching, or like highly effective professional learning communities. Sometimes that growth comes from attending presentations or workshops on local, regional, or national stages. There are lots of pathways for growth, thankfully, and lots of teacher leaders in this arena doing the work to nurture that growth.

Strategies to Turn Growth into Greatness

If you are passionate about rejecting the failing status quo, you need to stand up and step up to create better learning experiences for teachers. Whether you want one-on-one experiences or the opportunity to guide a larger team, here are some essential skills you can put to work that will allow teachers to develop, evolve, and strengthen their craft at the highest levels.

Practice Servant Leadership

The first step in becoming a world-class developer of others is realizing it isn't about you—not even a little bit. We can't overstate how tricky this realization is. Chances are, you are a great person to lead professional development specifically because of your immense skill in the classroom. The very things that got you here are now to be set aside so you can focus on others. That is hard! You might still be able to share a critical insight or put a teacher in touch with the perfect resource, but your goal is to shine a light on another's journey and to help illuminate that person's pathway to greatness.

It's not easy to set aside your own personal ego, pride, or accomplishments, but it's vital that you give up your hold on them. When you try to assist others by constantly referencing your own successes or journey, it forever tethers their growth to yours. It makes *comparison* a focus instead of your colleague's own valid and unique experiences. Honor others by setting aside your story so that you can attend to theirs. One way to make sure you stay on track is to observe the following mantra: "Whatever you need, however you need it, whenever you need it." It takes a hero's effort to stay selfless and to keep giving in the service of your colleagues, but this is how people grow and guide others.

Build Relationships

We spoke in Chapter 2 about the idea of meeting people where they are. If this isn't the most potent idea of all time, in education or anywhere, we really don't know what is. It applies to learners of all ages and levels. When it comes to offering professional development or coaching others in their craft, it's no different. We know that not every teacher wants to be coached, not every teacher is comfortable with a coaching relationship, and not every teacher has consented to coaching. Conversely, some educators adore the idea and are wide open to the possibility of being seen and getting better with help. Job one is to discover the disposition of the teacher you have been asked to work with and build your relationship from there.

If resistance is the starting point, find out what kinds of things the teacher is proud of or good at and work from there. Find out if there's something that person has always wanted to try but needed more hands-on-deck assistance to get off the ground. Offer yourself up as one who could provide those hands. If you are welcomed with open arms, ask what areas of growth your colleague might like to take on and go from there. Whatever the scenario, as you build trust, it's important that you talk about feedback too. Negotiate whether or not your teacher would like feedback from you, in what form, and how often. Developing teachers is a lot like dancing: once you agree to join hands and dance, you still have to navigate all the rest of the steps together.

Listen to Learn

If you develop teachers, you learn very quickly how important the art of listening becomes. It's so vital, say Laura Lipton and Bruce Wellman in *Mentoring Matters* (2003), that it can "form the foundation for mutual learning and future exploration. Giving our full attention to a colleague contributes to the learning relationships and to clear communication" (p. 37). Listening is one of the most significant things you can do when you want to assist other people in their own growth. When you sit with your colleague to talk about teaching and learning, ask open-ended questions like "What was your aim with this lesson?" "What surprised you?" "What went well?" "What would you do differently?" Then listen very carefully to the responses. Use those responses as the way into a deeper conversation that will start to light up pathways toward improvement. You can ask one of our favorite questions: "On a scale of 1 to 10, how would you rate this lesson/activity/student product?" Then, when they answer, ask (if the score is less than 10), "What one or two things might you have done to increase that score?" If the teacher says it's a 10 out of 10, ask, "What are one or two things you saw that confirm this was a home-run lesson?" When teachers start to answer the questions you ask, they get a rare opportunity to do some thinking out loud. These verbalizations help you know where to go next and help them reflect on and solidify teaching behaviors worth repeating.

Find Opportunities to Model the Process and Scaffold to Guarantee Success

When you work with teachers to try new things or improve an existing practice, it's valuable to demonstrate it first while they watch. Often teachers are afraid to try something that they've never done before, especially in front of someone else. Do whatever you can to help reduce that fear. Typically that involves doing a demonstration lesson with students once on your own and then coteaching it with the teacher at least two more times. Then watch the teacher try it again one or two more times before meeting together to discuss how it went. You also want to scaffold for success by creating a series of fail-safe steps, materials, and resources that the teacher can use so that, if necessary, a lifeline is nearby. You want teachers to be able to focus on teaching and learning. The less they have to worry about what to do next or where to go to get support or resources, the more likely the professional development will be successful.

Stick Around

Some of the best moments in professional development happen after you've delivered the goods, so it's important to stick around. New questions and worries crop up that you can work on together, deepening your professional bond. The teachers you've worked with are often ready to go out on a proverbial limb and try something bold and new because you gave them the confidence to do so. Make yourself available for the moment when these teachers want to accelerate their effort; then watch your colleagues fly with the confidence and skill you've painstakingly helped them develop.

Cameron McKinley found herself in this exact position when a teacher she'd been working with sought her out for help with an exciting, cutting-edge (for her) classroom activity:

> In the schools I serve, we use Google Apps for education. Every student has a Chromebook they use for schoolwork and study. I worked with a high school English teacher who was very tied to the lab and used it frequently because it was a comfortable scenario for her. She could see every screen and monitor the whole class at once. She was resisting using her one-on-one Chromebooks and entering into the "shared document" situation with kids. She just wasn't certain enough about how it would work to feel confident to make the switch.
>
> I did the same things with her that I do with my students when I want them to try something new. I let her go at her own pace and didn't force her to do anything, just made myself available to support her when she was ready. Eventually she saw other teachers using Google Docs for collaboration and how they were able to give live feedback to improve [students'] writing while they were still in the process of drafting. She came to me and said,

"I want to try this." We created a Google classroom for her students, and I showed her how to assign and receive work. As we learned together, she was excited to be able to "see" kids while they were working. She noticed something else that was interesting: kids who were too afraid to raise their hands and ask for help in front of others were suddenly, easily asking for help. She could see learning occurring more clearly and had a written history of their questions, revisions, and feedback. Their engagement spiked too. I think that by the time we were fully operational, she realized that sometimes the biggest changes are the really easy ones. The biggest leap she had to make was being willing to take the risk.

When I checked back in with her to follow up, our relationship truly blossomed. Gone was the fear, and in its place, excitement and curiosity. She was so pumped about how her class had changed, she wanted to teach me about Breakout.edu, a logic game–based classroom activity where students solve challenges together to open a series of locks. I came in and we had a breakout activity. I did two breakouts for her class, but then I coached her to think about how kids could get into this project more centrally. We've moved from collaboration docs for writing, to interactive learning activities, to having her students create their own breakout puzzles for others. The door is wide open now, and I have no doubt she will continue to explore ways to use technology to enhance teaching and learning.

Use Adult-Learning Techniques

Part of the reason so many teacher-development initiatives fail is because of the way they are presented to teachers. We are all experts at knowing our students and the science of how kids learn best, but too often those same kid-centric practices are used to teach teachers. This is where things can go so wrong. In 1970, scholar Malcolm Knowles posited the theory of "andragogy," the science of how adults learn best. This theory reminded us, among other things, that "adults are almost always voluntary learners, and they simply disappear from learning experiences that don't satisfy them" (p. 54). This concept, along with several others that make up the full definition of andragogy, is required learning for anyone hoping to help teachers grow their craft and practice. Keep in mind the following tenets:

- Adults want their time and expertise honored. They want to bring this expertise to the learning situation and use the new knowledge to help enrich or improve their existing practice.
- Adults need to see that new ideas or ways of doing things work well before adopting them. Be prepared with several successful examples of what you want them to try.
- Adults want time to engage with, practice, and apply new techniques as well as time to reflect on and discuss the work they are doing to determine the relevance of it to their practice.
- Adults want commitment. Too often, schools abandon ship before waiting to see the successes of the work they do. Teachers know how long it takes to learn and implement something well (years). It's demoralizing to see how quickly we shift to the next big thing before we've gotten good at what is in front of us. Instead, adults appreciate a slower, more methodical rollout of new ideas, strategies, curriculum, or experiences.
- Adults crave strong facilitators and expert guides who can help them with short- and long-range goal setting along with continuous and routine check-ins to examine student work and data to determine progress.

Employing practices that incorporate these tenets increases the likelihood of a powerful outcome. Steady, relevant, and respectful advancement with teachers is a strategy that always wins the race.

Know the *Why*

No matter what you are working on, be able to articulate the reason or reasons you are asking a teacher to do something. As we learned from Simon Sinek's much-viewed TED talk on vision, "People don't care *what* you do, they care *why* you do it" (2009). This statement is as true for kids in classrooms as it is for teachers. We are bombarded constantly with questions to answer, problems to solve, new tasks to complete, phone calls and e-mails to answer, lessons to plan. Every minute of a teacher's day is gobbled up, so convincing a teacher to try something new just because you said so isn't going to work. You've got to lead with *why*.

Whenever you meet with teachers, remind them of your shared mission to increase student achievement and create meaningful learning experiences for kids. If you know the teacher and understand the kinds of things that matter most to her, speak to that passion as well. Grounding your work together in a powerful reason *why* is like adding gas to the tank. You'll go far on that fuel. For Josh Parker, it's an ethics issue:

> The ability to push teachers on behalf of kids is hard, but I have to do it. Improving outcomes for black and brown kids is essential. I can't turn my back on that. There is a real and significant harm that will come to children if they cannot read and know literacy at high levels. Conveying the urgency of the matter to other educators, in as positive and open a way as possible, brings them into the *why* as a partner in important ways. Difficult conversations can happen when we understand the *why* together.

Honor Voice, Choice, and Agency

Whenever possible, give teachers a voice and some choices about how your professional development relationship will roll out. Negotiate when and how you will meet, how long these meetings will last, what kinds of work you might do together during that time, and what an appropriate goal or target might be to signal that progress is being made. Giving teachers some agency about the inquiry work you are going to do together increases trust, decreases resistance, and helps to dissipate fear. There may be occasions during your work together when you must direct the proceedings. That's completely normal. As long as the relationship has a sense of give and take, you're on the right track.

As Rebecca began her work with instructional leadership teams at the secondary level, she began to see the power that personalization and choice had on the process of growing teacher leadership skills. No longer forced to implement something the district had selected for them, teachers themselves got to assess the greatest needs at their sites and then figure out the best way to address them.

Once each team had selected a sitewide focus, Rebecca and her colleagues began to work together to create a year of learning for teachers. Each team needed to determine several things: how they would roll out their idea to colleagues, what kinds of activities and experiences teachers would want to have, and how they could assess their starting point and collect evidence and artifacts to show growth by the end of the year. At every meeting that year, they spent the morning working on coaching and leadership development activities for the team, and in the afternoon the teams would break up and work on how to deliver professional development and use their coaching skills back at their sites. They also spent time in conversational protocols to think through unique issues or struggles each site was experiencing. It was just as important that the team charged with doing the work had exposure to new learning and growth opportunities as it was for those who would be on the receiving end of the coaching.

At sites, teams were responsible for delivering instruction and sharing strategies with their colleagues at after-school faculty meetings and specially scheduled trainings. Each school followed its own pathway, but the work included demonstration lessons, guest speakers, rubric-calibration workshops, surveys, student work analyses, instructional rounds, data analysis, and presentations by the teachers at the end of the year. At one school, the Instructional Leadership Team (ILT) members were given release time to visit teachers for coteaching opportunities or to meet together to plan lessons or review student work. At another school, teachers were allowed to request members of the ILT to come to their classrooms to assist in implementing the ideas and strategies that were part of their focus for the year. At the third school, where there were five focus groups, each team received special collaboration time to meet together to chart and monitor their journeys with the assistance of one of the ILT members.

Not only were teachers receiving something radical and new—ongoing onsite support for their development work—but the instructional leaders were receiving the same help maintaining their own momentum. This kind of personalized, coordinated, and teacher-run professional development was a 180-degree turnaround from any professional development endeavors their district had taken on for years.

Let Your Kids' Work Lead the Way

When developing professional development for a teacher or for groups of teachers, it's natural to focus on teaching practices, curricular choices, or student behavior. However, as John Hattie's (2012) research on "visible learning" so clearly demonstrates, it's teachers' understanding of their impact on learners that offers the best chance for growth and improvement.

Knowing a teacher's impact starts by looking at student work. When you come together, try to make student work samples the focus of your conversations. Ask questions such as these: (1) "What were you teaching that resulted in this student work?" (2) "What do you see when you look at these products?" (3) "What were you hoping to see from students?" (4) "Do you see that here, and if so, how well is it done? If not, why not?" (5) "What might you do differently to get a different result next time?"

In conversations that put student work at the center, two things happen. First, we get a student-facing view of the teaching that differs from the view that emerges when asking teachers how they felt a lesson went. So many times we are more critical of our teaching than is warranted. We've all had a lesson we felt was unsuccessful but resulted in terrific student work that didn't mesh with our internal assessment. We've also had days we felt were total winners, but student work and feedback didn't measure up. The clearest metric for how well we're doing can and should be from the students themselves. Starting with their work helps begin the conversation in the right way. The second thing that happens when student work is the centerpiece of the conversation is that defensiveness is minimized. Talking about students, their efforts, and what we see puts most teachers into an empathetic, curious state of mind, one where a search for strengths and answers is the focus. We often speak more carefully and thoughtfully about our students than about ourselves, and it's in this kinder place that personal growth has a chance to take root.

Combine Your Talents and Know Your Stuff

When you do any kind of work to grow teachers, you need to be firing on every cylinder because your clients and audiences come to you with formidable expectations. It's not enough to reach into the toolbox to grab what you know works in the classroom; you'll need to supplement your skillset with several other talents.

Start by making sure you are steeped in your content so that questions from any angle don't throw you. Stockpile several examples of lessons you've taught, successes you've witnessed, and hurdles and bumps in the road to anticipate, so that no matter what comes up, you have an example to support your work. Begin developing a strong memory, because working with adults demands that you know not just your content, but a vast array of educational research. Being able to pluck a fact or statistic from the research means you've got to have quick access to all that you know. This is no easy feat, but it's a hallmark of every great developer of teachers.

In any given lesson, you might have one or two objectives for the period, and the same might be true for coaching, delivering professional development, or presenting on a wider stage. However, when your audience is teachers, you need to be prepared for the direction of your work to shift if that's what the participants need. Be flexible and as accommodating as you can manage without turning your own psyche upside down. You'll also need emotional intelligence and the ability to read the people in the room carefully and correctly. Laugh, listen, and engage with your audience, but also press on and don't let side conversations or small challenges divert you. Celebrate victories and accomplishments while you work, and pay close attention to energy levels—yours and theirs. Take breaks and give teachers sandbox time or processing time. Bake in time for teachers to talk about what they're learning. That's how the learning filters down and settles inside.

Finally, be authentic. You are human. You think, you feel, you love, you hurt. So does everyone in your audience. People learn best from those they feel a connection to, whatever that connection is, so don't hesitate to share stories from your life and from your classroom. Tell the tales of your students. Welcome your audience into your world just as you are hoping they'll allow you and your ideas into theirs. This human transaction is powerful and a great medium for growth.

Push Back Positively

Any learning process will include some conflict. When you are delivering content to educators or taking them through a workshop, there will be teachers who resist, who don't agree, or who want to challenge you. It's often said that teachers make the worst students. During professional development sessions, they multitask, socialize constantly, and criticize quickly if they believe something isn't relevant to them. So although describing teachers as "the worst students" might cause a chuckle, that reaction is not warranted if you take the time to remember actual times when colleagues shared how stressful a professional development experience was. Professional development can honestly be traumatic for some people, and that reaction is something you need to plan for. After all, it's normal to expect students to give teachers grief occasionally, but somehow such a response is more alarming and frustrating when it's coming from teachers themselves.

First, resist the temptation to lash out or lose your temper—which can be difficult to do. Stay calm, stay positive, pause to collect your thoughts, and push back gently only after you've listened to the concern and sorted out its genesis. Is it more information they need? Then give it. Is it research they're aware of that differs from what you were aware of? Then admit that and accept it. Is it a challenge about whether or not something will work? Then share examples where you have seen success. Whatever the moment requires, try your best to deliver it. Sometimes the answer is "I don't know"—and that's perfectly OK. Do what you might do with your students and model the process of discovering answers together. Throw it out to the audience and seek information. Add what is shared to what you know in an attempt to answer the question. When no answers emerge, ask the group if you might table that topic or put a pin in it for later, and then—no matter what—return to it even if it's to say you still don't have the answers. Commit yourself to finding the answers and sharing your findings as soon as possible.

Josh recounts a moment during day one of the Los Angeles Standards Institute, a five-day intensive program created and run by UnboundEd, designed to show teachers how to teach rigorous standards-based lessons to all children without exception, thus ensuring equity around learning:

> Basically, we cook 'em. We put these smart folks from all over the country in a room for five eight-hour days straight. We give them the latest research, great instruction, keynotes, and collaborative conversation that change them. It sets the stage for improving pathways for black and brown kids in stark and semi-aggressive ways. At the end, they come out different, but not without a fair amount of struggle along the way.
>
> When you are dealing with adults on topics that are this sensitive, you need to be aware of and ready for backlash. In my work with the institutes, I've had to engage more aggressively around the backlash than I ever have before. I can't shy away, not when it comes to who does and who doesn't get to access quality literature or knowledge. Whereas in a classroom I might choose to address something a child brings up privately, away from the whole class, in an institute, I have to do it right there in front of everyone.
>
> Recently I had a teacher who did not like the fact that we were telling teachers that they should do complex texts with kids who cannot read. He thought this was a good theory, but in practice, he wasn't so sure it would work.
>
> Before I said a word, I had to hear what he was saying. The heartbreak I had to hide was that [this] teacher was challenging the research that shows when children are given access to high-quality, foundational texts along with the scaffolds to support their understanding, their lives and trajectories change for the better. My heart was pounding because I needed to push my hurt aside so I could answer without disrespecting him. I listened. I validated his thinking but pushed back. I asked, "What's the cost of doing nothing? If we don't do this, what's the end result?" I used personal examples from my own life and the lives of my students. I talked about how when my students took standardized tests, the texts were so difficult many kids just gave up and walked out. Having kids drop out of the learning process is the cost of doing nothing. Teachers should not be OK with being part of a system that allows that lack of support for, or belief in, kids.

All the while, I had to keep my voice level. I had to be pleasant. I could not get upset or perturbed. Why? Because we are grappling with enormous systemic issues on a profound and personal level. I've done the work. I know what's at stake. He was still trying to work it through. My job was to keep him open and willing to continue on the journey and to have plenty of strategies for how we unravel these challenges together.

Professional Development Pitfalls and How to Avoid Them

Teachers trade war stories about professional development. They really do. And it's no wonder: year after year, with the best of intentions, we nearly bore teachers to death with soul-sucking sit-and-get talk-a-thons. Providing high-quality, actionable professional development requires a commitment to doing things differently and treating teachers as active, enthusiastic learners. It's a huge responsibility and one you must get just right. The following tips will help you ensure your PD sessions get talked about afterward for all the right reasons.

Undervaluing Experience

When mentoring, coaching, or teaching teachers, there's a real danger in undervaluing their experience. You might have more years of service or skill, or more accolades and a title, but if you aren't careful, this pitfall can throw off the balance of the relationship. Combining that danger with too much focus on getting teachers to do something or produce something different than they did before makes them feel like objects and tools instead of valued experts. That combination is a recipe for shutdown.

Remember, all teachers have wisdom and expertise, and all learning is a process. When you enter a relationship with teachers, you must come to it as equals and as a vulnerable member of a partnership that will grow together. Learning to harness the power and passion of those you work with and adding to it your own unique ideas for growth in humane and respectful ways are key.

Expecting a Quick Pace of Change

Once you leave the classroom to coach teachers or work on large-scale district initiatives, you'll realize that change at this scale is smaller to see and harder to detect. But the change is still there. Classroom teachers are accustomed to seeing their direct impact on kids on a daily basis, so when the change is more incremental, it can be demoralizing and they might feel as if they're accomplishing nothing at all.

Don't despair. Don't shift gears. Avoid creating urgencies that can strangle the real, sustainable (if small) changes that are taking hold. Remember that if a ship moves a fraction of an inch off course, it will eventually travel to an entirely new destination. It might not seem as if you're doing much good. You are. Be patient.

Overloading Teachers

To engage successfully in professional development, you have to think a lot like a teacher. You need to know your audience well and scaffold anything you want them to learn or do uniquely for them, just as you would for your students. You might be providing something simple for one teacher and working at the cutting-edge level with another. If you don't calibrate that difference carefully, you risk overloading people. We have definitely seen people be scared off by a coach who moved too fast or a professional development session that covered content not relevant to the teachers in the room. You don't want to lose someone you are trying to help, because the reality is you might never get that person back. Similarly, you need to make sure your district can "clear the decks" so that, to whatever degree possible, teachers are expected during the professional development experience to do nothing else except the work of getting better. This expectation is mighty tricky as new standards, curriculum adoptions, and district mandates make it difficult to focus entirely on what you're setting out to do. Guarantee you have a shot by removing as many needless distractions from teachers' plates as possible.

Watering the Rocks

We hate to say this, but there are some teachers who are immune to improvement. They have become burnt out, are ineffectual without realizing it, or worse, actively torpedo efforts to grow themselves.

Don't water the rocks. Ignore them. You can't help them anyway. Instead, feed the hungry. Work with the teachers who want to grow, who are willing to stay on a path of continuous improvement. Convince your administrators to do the same. Too many districts spend time and money enforcing seat-time requirements or impose administrative itineraries on professional development sessions or PLCs to keep teacher groups accountable. Instead, plan for and activate your *best* teachers. The energy and momentum they generate can be enough to destabilize—in a good way—a staff that appears to be stuck in place. The good teachers truly want to be more like the great ones, and the bad ones eventually realize they're outnumbered. It's better to have the misfits unhappy rather than your teacher rock stars, as the latter can do more to help your school reach its goals and grow.

Creating Dependencies

Some sage and radical advice we once heard was that great leaders work to put themselves out of a job as fast as they can. Sounds crazy, right? But nestled within this idea is the seed of empowerment and scale. If coaches or leaders of professional development never build the skill or confidence in teachers to enable them to continue on their own path to greatness without the coach, then all that's been created is a chain of dependency that does not advance the teachers' practice. We've seen that happen in many places where outstanding teacher leaders have incredible ideas and so much passion to make great things happen but lack the ability to stand beside their coached colleagues and tease these qualities and confidence out of them. Teacher development is tough work, and not everyone can do it well. It requires selfless souls who care more about making sure teachers can do things well on their own and who take great pride and confidence when that happens and they are no longer needed. *That* indicates a job well done.

Lessons Learned by—and from—Cameron, Rebecca, and Josh

At the start of this chapter we presented three teachers who discovered needs in their systems that were not being filled. Cameron had professional expertise from her first career with IBM and the Air Force that could easily and immediately be brought to teachers and classrooms to make life better for everyone. Rebecca felt an almost rebellious desire to undo the damage of 20 years of poorly implemented professional development, if given the chance. Josh felt a personal calling to get into the heart of the national conversation around achievement for kids of color and work to repair the damage that decades of low expectations have done to American children. All three of them created a pathway for diving in and doing the work they knew mattered most in order to help other educators grow.

Cameron learned how truly helpful it was to marry her skills in the private and public sectors with her coaching work. Seeing teachers as clients, listening to their needs and desires, identifying solutions, and then moving slowly toward them together created safe spaces for both teachers and students to learn and grow. She saw that a trusting relationship with her teachers was at the heart of every good experience. She even got to bring the "customer is always right" mentality to situations when she didn't have the answers. As she explains,

> I understood right away that my best coaching moments came when I watched and listened to my colleagues. I became a better asker of questions and of getting to the essence of what a teacher's desires or fears were. Developing this open channel of communication, and trust, [was] necessary for growth to happen. It even helped when I didn't know the answer to a teacher's question or the best method to solve a problem.
>
> I tried never to be intimidated when I didn't know something. Instead, I would be honest about it and say, "Let's find out together," or even better, I'd allow those around me, including our students, to teach me. It's an amazing confidence builder when students, or teachers you've been coaching, get to turn the tables on the mentor and show her a thing or two. It also sets a strong example of having a growth mindset myself and being open to learning new things. It's important to never lose touch of what it feels like to not

know how to do something or to be unsure. Finding low-risk ways to build knowledge and skill and then offering many opportunities to practice these new skills were the way we moved forward together.

Rebecca's journey to transforming professional learning for her colleagues started by honoring the people in the room. So often choices about what teachers learn are made by people who think they know but who are actually pretty far removed from teachers' daily needs and struggles. Step one was asking teachers what they wanted and then finding a way to make it happen.

Every teacher in the group Rebecca was working with had talent and experience that could be respected and harnessed. She knew from her own experiences that at this stage of her career, there are very few experts who had all the answers she was seeking. She had her own wisdom and body of knowledge about what works and what doesn't in the classroom and with teachers. Realizing that all of her colleagues were experienced and had ideas about what they wanted meant that her role as a growth agent was to invite them to the content she was sharing and then to ask them to determine how it would fit in with what they knew about teaching and learning. The conversations with the teams were studies in intellectual negotiation and some of the most powerful moments of their time together.

Through her experience of working with teachers to cultivate their professional development pathways, Rebecca found it abundantly clear that they had the skill and passion to drive their projects successfully; they just needed to be given the opportunity and trusted to drive the process. After sharing a wide array of research on John Hattie's (2012) work around visible learning, on working with adult learners (Knowles, 1970), on school culture and climate, on teachers' will and skill drivers, and on creating 21st century learning experiences for teachers, it was time for teams to decide their course of action.

Rebecca asked the instructional leadership teams this question: "Given all that you have learned so far, given your students, your school culture, and the teachers you work with, what is it you'd like *your* school and your teachers to focus on this year?" Teams spent time thinking through what aspects of teacher development they wished to embark on and set a focus for the year.

The middle school teams had the easiest time selecting what they wished to do. One chose to have teachers focus on implementing Universal Design for Learning (UDL) practices in every classroom on their campus. Another middle school team chose to increase their student population's writing scores by teaching the entire staff about their school's writing curriculum and bringing all non–English language arts teachers onto the same page about it. The third middle school opted for more of a "genius hour" idea with their plan. They presented five powerful practices from the Hattie (2012) research and allowed teachers at their site to select their own focus for growth for the year. Once the teams set a focus and a goal for their work, Rebecca watched what happened with a sense of pure awe and the realization that letting strong teachers lead enables remarkable things to happen.

Perhaps the most stunning discovery was something Rebecca saw after the work was well underway, something that is supported by the research done by Roland Barth (2004) around teacher development through powerful professional development collaborations. Barth says,

> When teachers are given the chance to sharpen their iron with the help of their colleagues, [they] win something important. They experience a reduction in isolation; the personal and professional satisfaction that comes from improving their schools; a sense of instrumentality, investment, and membership in the school community; and new learning about schools, about the process of change, and about themselves. And all of these positive experiences spill over into their classroom teaching. These teachers become owners and investors in the school, rather than mere tenants. They become professionals. (p. 449)

Rebecca saw the teachers in her district become newly engaged and invigorated in the work of teaching. So many teachers at every site shared their gratitude for being trusted and respected enough to do this work. This excitement was most evident in how it inspired teachers who may not have been on the official instructional leadership team to step up and take on the work. Teachers who had never been given a choice or a chance were suddenly spending every free minute researching feedback strategies or means of representation and sharing their findings with their principals and colleagues. They were rising to fill the shoes of a teacher leader in ways that had never before been open to them.

As teachers worked through the year, their conversations about teaching and student learning prompted new discoveries, new questions, and new interests. With the freedom to move in the direction the work took them, teachers were more motivated than ever to understand their students and how they could best serve them. Imagine working at a school where teachers are consumed by understanding their effectiveness and working hard to get better at doing what they love: teaching. This new direction for personalized, focused professional development achieved just that.

For Josh, participating in UnboundEd's Standards Institutes has been a humbling honor, and yet one of the greatest challenges of his life. Not only is the content and crux of the work of paramount importance for the teaching profession, but also the skills required to pull it off with authority and humanity are massive. The challenge has forced Josh to weave together and activate nearly every skill and talent he has with every bit of knowledge and experience he possesses. Here's how he describes his experience:

> Through the institutes I have worked with teachers, administrators, superintendents, assistant superintendents, and nonprofit directors from Florida, California, Louisiana, Michigan, the District of Columbia, and my home state of Maryland. We are together for eight hours a day, five days in a row. Adults need time to process and understand this idea that equity can live, even thrive, in a standards-based curriculum. It's a bit of a pressure cooker, a brutal experience, but a really necessary one, and the stamina I need to do it well is key. The rigor of the week is new for me as a teacher leader. When I teach a full load of classes to kids, that's rigorous too, but when I do institutes, I don't really have breaks. I am on for three hours straight, teaching this content, I have one [hour] off while a co-presenter works, then three more when I'm back at it again. "Lather-rinse-repeat" for five days.
>
> [Gathering] the volume of research I have to have ready at any given time is a skill that stretches my ability to present. I have to be at my peak and be able to access information quickly, authoritatively, and with some brevity

as well because we don't have time for long-winded recaps of scholarly findings. So it's got to be quick but the right information for the moment.

When I teach a lesson for kids, I get to choose one to two objectives, so I get to manage the content and volume of any given day. At Unbound, you have several objectives often working simultaneously. If [teachers] gets stuck or confused, or if they aren't familiar with the texts we work with, I have to be able to stop to teach it to them quickly and concisely. There are very immediate, very real, very unique challenges to presenting this kind of content for teachers in this setting. And hey! It's all while discussing the most uncomfortable topic in the nation and maintaining a positive disposition while talking about how we can optimistically solve the challenges before us.

The emotional and intellectual weight of the work, the pressure on my memory, the preparation before, during, and after these presentations, as well as the rigor of the week make this kind of teacher development work the most challenging I've ever done. It's not for the faint of heart, and it's not, in a practical sense, for everyone. But there are people out there who are unique, who *do* have these skillsets, who are special. Those folks change the world.

All of us work alongside wonderful colleagues who are doing their absolute most to make their students' days meaningful, relevant, and challenging. It's inspiring to see all that we do for and give our students. But who teaches the teachers? Who is out there inspiriting, guiding, and growing us? That is the vacuum that desperately needs to be filled. With these strategies, the teacher stories, and knowledge about the pitfalls to avoid, you can begin to fill this gap and help grow the village of teachers to greatness.

4

Map Reading 101: Understanding and Using Research and Data to Strengthen Your Work

Some of the best theorizing comes after collecting data because then you become aware of another reality.

—Robert J. Shiller

Daniele Massey is the 2013 United States Department of Defense Teacher of the Year. Teaching in a military setting has provided her with a unique perspective. She understands what it's like to work with students who are transient, who struggle to deal with loss, and who don't feel like they fit in. The students in her school have a high mobility rate. Imagine what it feels like for students who are constantly on the move trying to make friends. Consider the pain children carry to school every day as they secretly hold back the emotion that comes with a parent being deployed into combat.

Daniele and one of her colleagues conducted a study for their school improvement team. The results of their research revealed a major problem. African American boys at the high school were failing algebra at an alarming rate. The two teachers realized there was a flaw in the system that was inhibiting student learning. How could Daniele and her colleague discover the root of the problem and develop a possible solution?

Derek Olson, the 2008 Minnesota State Teacher of the Year, is the kind of junior high teacher that students love. He has spent more than 25 years designing authentic learning experiences, such as a playground archaeologist dig, to tap into the unbridled energy of young students. He is constantly on the lookout for new ways to connect his 6th grade social studies class to the world.

Content to work with students, Derek didn't see himself as an educational advocate. However, a trip to the Minnesota State Senate flipped his world upside down. While there, Derek was filled with frustration as he listened to a senator discuss the positive impact a bill would have on the teacher evaluation process. According to Derek, "The testimony was filled with inaccuracies and would do great harm to public education." He was left with the unenviable choice of saying nothing and watching the bill pass or standing up and challenging a senator. What skills and knowledge did he have to make a difference?

Teaching in a rural school district in Wisconsin, Leah Luke, the 2010 Wisconsin State Teacher of the Year, was far removed from high-level education policy discussions in the nation's capital. There was little time to ponder the big picture at the federal level. Instead, like all good teachers, Leah poured her efforts into the students in her classroom. It was a realm in which she excelled.

An invitation to attend the annual meeting of the Education Commission of the States was about to extend Leah's sphere of influence in ways she never dreamed possible. The event was packed with policymakers and stakeholders. As she describes it,

> What struck me as odd was the small number of teachers who were in attendance. Approximately 33 State Teachers of the Year were guests of the organization. The power the people at the event had to make decisions that would impact classrooms in schools across the country was staggering. However, as a profession, teachers had little representation. The other State Teachers of the Year who were in attendance felt the same. During that year, I became frustrated with how little policymakers appeared to listen to us.

What could one teacher from rural Wisconsin do to make a difference on the national stage?

Daniele, Derek, and Leah were all confronted with big issues that at first glance had no easy solutions. It would have been easy for each of them to throw their hands up in the air in frustration, walk away, and leave the issues for someone else to solve. Thankfully, they did not. Instead, all three learned how to conduct research and use the collected data to become change agents.

Over the past several decades, the term *data* has been given a bad rap in the teaching profession. It has become the primary weapon for the attack on the perceived poor quality of education in U.S. schools. In 1983 a study entitled *A Nation at Risk* was published by President Ronald Reagan's National Commission on Excellence in Education. The report launched a tidal wave of interest in America's international ranking in education. A serious version of the blame game followed. Classroom teachers were caught in the middle of the finger-pointing crossfire. Students and teachers felt helpless as assessments and data consumed them. New evaluation models were tied to student test scores, but few educators were appropriately trained on how to collect and analyze data to improve instruction. Feelings of helplessness grew as America's teachers found themselves floating on a raft of negativity while lost in a sea of data.

The good news is that things are starting to shift. Teachers and administrators are starting to understand how data can be used to improve instruction, celebrate student achievement, and rewrite the narrative about what constitutes great teaching and learning. The change in mindset has transformed a perceived threat into a powerful tool. Now we have opportunities to learn how to identify problems in our classrooms or schools, understand the nuances behind how information is collected and shared, and understand how we can use the data we find to take the steps needed to solve some of our biggest challenges.

However, teacher confidence on the use of data remains a stumbling block, according to a report from the U.S. Department of Education (Means, Chen, DeBarger, & Padilla, 2011). The study showed that the use of data in the decision-making process was tied directly to how confident a teacher felt in having the ability to analyze and interpret the information.

This chapter will provide you with real-life examples of how teachers use data to create meaningful change. It also offers a series of action steps to help you develop new skills that will increase your confidence in data, as well as related pitfalls to avoid.

Strategies for Improving Instruction with Research and Data

Research and data are two of the most powerful tools that are readily available to teachers. Unfortunately, many teachers fail to recognize those tools' ability to help them create compelling arguments that they can use as levers to promote change on a grand scale. The following strategies will help you develop your research skills and learn how to use data to support your work.

Identify the Problem

Problems come in all different shapes and sizes. Take time to identify what, exactly, the issue is. One of the best ways to do so is to focus on *why* you believe there is an issue. Japanese industrial engineer and businessman Taiichi Ohno incorporated a process called the "5 Whys" into his work to help refine the manufacturing production system for Toyota Motor Corporation (Nakane & Hall, 2002). The number *5* is significant because that is the number of iterations he used to help boil the problem down to a single cause.

Here's an example of how a teacher leader might use the process to identify a problem. According to an article in *USA Today* (O'Donnell & Saker, 2018), teen suicide rates have increased 70 percent from 2006 to 2016. Schools are facing growing pressure to take a harder look at issues like student depression and anxiety. The 5 Whys could help a teacher leader determine why students might be struggling with those issues at their school:

- **Why** are so many students struggling with severe depression and anxiety? *Because they feel like they are all alone and have no friends.*
- **Why** do students feel isolated? *Because many lack confidence and the necessary skills to build successful relationships.*

- **Why** do students lack the requisite skills to build relationships? *Because many do not have access to people who can help them develop those skills and grow relationships.*
- **Why** isn't the school doing more? *Because there is not a comprehensive program that provides teachers with the training, resources, and time to institute a program.*
- **Why** hasn't a program been developed? *Because the school's focus has been on academic standards and testing instead of developing a social and emotional learning program. That has been left up to individual teachers to address when they can.*

Once finished, the teacher leader can use this information to develop a proposal to share with colleagues and administrators so that they can discuss the importance of adding ongoing social and emotional learning to classrooms throughout the district.

This process will help you discover two things: Is there a problem? Are you asking the right question? You may discover during your journey that you have been focusing on the wrong issue. Some people find that situation frustrating. Don't! This is part of the process of elimination, which means you are well on your way to uncovering the real issue and one step closer to solving it.

Make Your Argument Using the Correct Form of Data

There are two types of data: quantitative and qualitative. *Quantitative* data is gathered and reported in numerical form. The focus of *qualitative* data is on what we observe and how we tell the story of what we saw. There is much discussion about which form of data paints a clearer picture and is therefore the most valuable. The correct answer is both. If you want to compare the number of times something occurred, then use quantitative data. However, if you are interested in developing a better understanding of the effect those instances had on students and staff, then look for qualitative data. Derek Olson encourages teachers to use the data that best meet their needs:

Looking back, I understand how qualitative and quantitative research methods are both important to the big picture. If the big numbers scare you, do qualitative research. The qualitative side of the equation enables researchers to assign faces to the numbers in order to create a powerful narrative. At the same time, concrete data is really important. If numbers speak to you, do quantitative research. There is a place for both. However, the most powerful study is when both qualitative and quantitative research support each other and flesh out a framework of really important information that we need to hear. Take the numbers to create the framework and use the anecdotal stories to paint the canvas. You'll have a piece of research art when you are done.

Don't forget to consider who you eventually plan to share the information with and what type of data will help sway their opinion. Do they need hard numbers, or are they more interested in the stories those numbers represent?

Start with the Big Data Picture

Once you have identified an issue that needs to be addressed and are ready to roll up your sleeves and get started on finding a solution, it's time to find out what the cause of the problem is. Where do you start? A lot of the data you need may have already been collected. One of the great things about schools is that they measure many things. Look at the big data picture that helps paint the overarching picture of what is being measured and start identifying the pieces of information you need to become better informed. For example, what do you know about the students who make up the data pool? How many students have IEPs? What is the racial composition? How many students are eligible for free or reduced lunch? Use the information that is easy to find to paint the first strokes of a comprehensive picture that tells the overall story. The school report card or school improvement plan is full of information. Meet with your team to identify all possible data sources. Generate a list and prioritize it by most to least relevant. Don't forget to consider the sensitivity of the data, and make sure to protect student and staff confidentiality. Discuss any questions you have regarding school code or laws that govern the use of data with either your building principal or union representative.

Lay out all the data sources you have and discuss them with your team. Develop a strategy for moving forward. There may be pieces of information that are not readily available or still need to be collected. Discuss how you want to do this. Surveys, focus groups, interviews, and observations are a few ways to collect information. Consider which methods will work best for your team.

Don't Forget to Look in the Mirror

The mirror is one of the last places people tend to look when trying to identify problems. In today's world, it's not easy to take responsibility. If you want to become a change agent who can lead a team of people to transform your learning environment, then personal accountability needs to become a well-used tool in your toolbox for success.

Everyone makes mistakes. However, very few people own them. Daniele Massey looked at her students' test scores one day and realized she was part of a much bigger problem that involved an inordinate number of African American boys failing algebra. Here's how she describes the situation:

> I began with examining my test scores to gain a better understanding of what was happening in my own classroom. I looked at a unit test and realized from the scores [that] some of my students just didn't get it. However, ready or not, they were forced to move on to the next unit. That's the way the system worked. Students were required to move on at the speed we set for them, not the other way around. By the end of the semester, the students who struggled came up to my desk and asked for extra credit. To them it was about the grade, not the skills. I knew something had to change.
>
> Another teacher and I created what we called "super-standards." At one point, we were asked to serve on the school improvement committee. During the process we really started digging into our school's test scores. We discovered a startling fact. A large section of our African American boys had failed Algebra I multiple times. There was a problem. Now, what could we do to fix it?

Daniele's willingness to look at the data, which led her to realize that some of her students were falling through the cracks, was a huge step in the right direction. She now "owned" the problem and started looking for the *whys* instead of trying to deflect the blame to someone else. In that moment, the students in her school gained a powerful ally who was one step closer to finding a solution.

Don't Let Fear Become a Stumbling Block

Let's face it: *research* and *data* are terms that in the past have been reserved for academia. The idea of conducting research and sifting through piles of data can be daunting. Derek Olson felt that way when he started his journey. His graduate work led to being asked to participate in a research study, but he was unsure about joining the project. As he explains,

> I lacked confidence, but the support of the project director led me to eventually agree to participate. I am so glad that I did. Being involved in the experience gave me the skills and confidence I would need later to meet with policymakers. There was also another valuable lesson in the experience: have faith when people recognize that you have a talent or skill to share on a project. Don't let a lack of confidence keep you from saying yes when others believe you have the skill to get the job done. If someone recognizes [your] potential to do something outside of [your] comfort zone, it's the time to take that step and grow.

Instead of fearing research and data, consider how you can use those tools to create positive change in your building or beyond. Teachers tend to complain about the lack of support they receive from administrators or policymakers. Unfortunately, a lot of the issues that are shared with administrators or policymakers come in the form of complaints that lack any form of concrete information or possible solutions. If the goal is to vent, then teachers shouldn't expect much in terms of resolution. However, well-researched issues that are accompanied by data-driven solutions are another matter. It's human nature to look for the nearest exit when a habitual complainer is spotted walking down the hallway. However, people who are problem solvers are valued and respected. Teachers in Finland are exemplary in this regard. They are highly respected, and research is an integral part of their culture

(Crouch, 2015). Consider the value that becoming a researcher can add to your practice. Start small and dream big on your research journey.

Listen to the Numbers

Well-conducted research can uncover amazing nuggets of information. Listen to the numbers. Don't let the glacial pace of education reform or the fact that someone in authority is married to a systemic method of instruction detour you from your path. At times, the data may be hard to accept. In Daniele Massey's case, the data showed the system was failing to meet the needs of African American boys. Here's what she and her colleagues found:

> The data showed us explicitly [that] the process of those students trudging along from unit to unit was not working. What good did it do to have them move to Unit 4 if they hadn't mastered the requisite skills in Unit 1? Furthermore, their scores on standardized tests that were given to measure student achievement in math showed those students had not mastered the necessary skills in 8th grade either. Our department meetings became a vicious cycle of finger pointing about who was responsible for what the students learned. That led to arguments as to whether the students should have learned the content in 6th or 7th grade. My point was that we were responsible for filling the holes in their learning. I reminded everyone there is a difference in teaching children who are connected with the military. At our school, we have a 33 percent turnover rate every year. There are other schools in our system that have a 97 percent turnover rate.

Daniele's findings may have been hard to accept. However, they were more difficult to ignore. The study led to a transformation in how instruction was delivered at her school. What issues are serving as roadblocks to stop progress at your school, and how can you use data to successfully deal with them?

Tell the Story of Student Success

Storytelling is the single most powerful tool in a teacher's toolbox for success, yet it remains largely unused. Think about how a simple

280-character tweet has the ability to move millions to tears or cheers by just a subtle change in context. The world loves stories. Parents and community members want to know what the students in your classroom are doing. They want to be connected. Unfortunately, not much storytelling happens in public education. Instead of full access into America's classrooms, the general public is left with only a snapshot from test scores or a negative post on social media from an angry parent. As a teacher, you have the ability to flip the paradigm upside down by sharing the amazing work students are doing in the classroom. Don't let a lack of self-confidence or fear of professional jealousy keep you from using this tool.

Leah Luke was frustrated with the lack of educator involvement in federal policy. She decided to apply for and was accepted to serve in the position of a teacher ambassador for the United States Department of Education. She was immediately given the opportunity to ensure that senior leadership in the department had access into the classroom. Here's her description of what her assignment involved:

> One of my jobs was to capture data regarding teacher efficacy through the use of anecdotal stories. Departmental staffers took the data we collected from the field and packaged it so leadership had a deeper understanding as to how people felt about education. One of the things we did was conduct roundtable discussions with teachers, professors, preservice teachers, and other stakeholders. We asked teachers to share what kept them up at night regarding public education. I captured the stories of people from Wisconsin, Minnesota, Illinois, and Ohio. It was gratifying to see each iteration of the stories as they came to life on a weekly basis. People's comments were funneled to the department. I felt like the stories were going somewhere and the interest from the department [was] sincere. People were really grateful about being able to have a conversation about education policy at that level.

Just like Leah, you can use storytelling to inform policymakers or shape public opinion. The big question is, what do you want people to know about your classroom or school? What media outlets do you have access to? At your next department meeting, generate a list of possible resources. The school Facebook page and website are great places to start. Content is king in the 21st century. Most content editors are starving for great stories. Talk with them to find out what the easiest way is to share information with them. If photographs are part of your story, make sure students have signed release forms to have their picture published. Also, make sure to find out what your district's policy is regarding how student names are shared. Some schools limit how much information can be posted in the digital space. Ask your content editor to provide feedback on what stories attract the most attention. You can use that information to help tailor how your stories are crafted. Don't forget to reach out to local media outlets like newspapers, radio stations, and television stations. Let your students talk to the media as much as possible. First, it's a great life experience for them. Second, the general public wants to hear from your students. Your school benefits from every positive story about education.

Seize the Moment to Present Your Findings

The last step in the research journey is to share your findings with the appropriate audience. This is where the rubber meets the road. It's the place where you make your case. How you present your findings can be just as important as the information you are sharing. Make sure to know your audience. Consider how the people you are sharing your data with will respond to it. Your research should be strong enough to stand on its own. However, think about what communication strategies you can use to maximize the impact of the information you are sharing. Work with your team to conduct practice sessions. Have someone on the team play the role of devil's advocate. Encourage that person to challenge your research. Consider filming the session and watching the video as a team to identify areas of the presentation that need improvement. Most important, know your research and be ready to share it on a moment's notice.

Derek Olson found himself in an unanticipated situation in the Minnesota Senate, where research he conducted from graduate school helped him challenge one of the state's leading policymakers. According to Derek,

I was in the senate with another teacher listening to testimony about an education bill on an evaluation tool. I wrote my dissertation on that tool and was keenly interested in the testimony. However, the more I listened to the conversation, the more frustrated I grew. The person who was there to assist in arranging visits to the different senate offices apparently saw the smoke coming out of my ears. He asked what was wrong. I told him that everything that was being shared about the evaluation tool was incorrect. He asked if I would like to testify. I jumped on the opportunity and said that I would talk to the author of the framework prior to my testimony.

I was scheduled to speak later that afternoon. The author called me prior to that time and shared how appalled she was about what Minnesota was considering. That call and the research I conducted on the topic for my dissertation provided me with both the confidence and ability to address lawmakers in the Minnesota Senate. Based on the data I collected, I had the ability to look the senators in the eye and say, "What you are planning to do is a complete misuse of the tool. Furthermore, the author of the framework you have proposed to use agrees that this state will be mired in lawsuits for the next 30 years if this bill goes through." At that point, a senator raised his hand and said, "Let me get this straight, Mr. Olson. Between this morning and now you were able to talk to the person who created this tool, and she told you it would be a bad idea for us to use it in this way?" I told him that was correct, and I told him why. I had the ability to share the data I had collected and why the tool could not be used with any degree of validity in the way they had proposed.

You could see [that] some senators who were opposed to the bill that I was arguing against wanted to stand up and cheer. Likewise, there were senators who could hardly wait for me to get out of that chair. I appreciated the opportunity to speak truth to power. The bill did not pass. I realize as a teacher leader that one of my roles is to continue to package and share the story of the impact policy has on student learning. The ability to conduct meaningful research has empowered me with the ability to do just that.

Teacher leaders understand how to conduct research and collect data in order to solve real-world issues. Never underestimate the power of well-conducted research in the hands of a master teacher to accomplish everything from changing curriculum at the district level to influencing federal policy.

Research and Data Pitfalls and How to Avoid Them

Used correctly, research and data can be a teacher's best friend. Unfortunately, a poorly designed research study can cause more damage than good. Attention to the following points will ensure you are headed in the right direction.

Making Things Harder Than They Need to Be

One way to derail your work is to make it too complicated. To avoid this pitfall—and to avoid a lot of confusion, frustration, and wasted time—lay out a plan. Write down the problem you are seeking to address at the top of a sheet of paper and try to answer the following questions: Who do you need on your team? When, where, and how often do you need to meet? What additional resources do you need to accomplish the task at hand? What data do you have available? Who are you trying to convince that something needs to change? Fill in as much information as you can. It's OK if you don't immediately have all the answers; the important thing is that you now have something that you can share with potential teammates. Don't forget to develop a pitch statement (see more about this in the next chapter). You'll use it to help encourage people to hop onboard with your project.

One of the first things you want to do as a team is to consider all the options you have available. Work together to develop a priority list and discuss what your next steps will be. Try to find the simplest solution to the problem. That doesn't mean you are looking for the easy way out. Quite the contrary. The point is that simple solutions typically require fewer resources, cause less disruption, and are more likely to be considered by those in charge.

Compromising the Integrity of Your Data

Make sure that your data are valid. If you can't find the answer to the problem, don't skew the research to support your point of view—or worse, fabricate data. Careers have been destroyed by such practices. The end result is not worth the risk, no matter how badly you want to see change occur. There is a difference between simplifying the process, as just suggested, and taking shortcuts. Make sure to cross the *t*s and dot the *i*s. Work with your team to develop a protocol for collecting data and ensuring the integrity of your work. The last thing you want to happen is for the legitimacy of your research to be questioned. By the way, that may be exactly what happens with topics that are extremely sensitive or if you are trying to sway the opinion of someone who is married to a certain practice. It's quite possible during your journey that you may meet people who are highly emotional, possess a fixed mindset, and are resistant to anything that is counter to their point of view. They may try to discredit your work. An adherence to a plan that ensures the integrity of your work is the best way to protect your name and move the work forward.

Failing to Give Credit to Others

Another surefire disaster is to take credit for someone else's work. Make sure to keep a record of resources you use and the people who offer assistance. One of the things you will learn through this journey is how much work goes into conducting solid research. You will gain a new respect for the time and energy and personal sacrifice others have put into their research. Discuss with your team the appropriate method to use to credit the work of others, and create a process for archiving that information so you have it when you need it.

Lessons Learned by—and from—Derek, Daniele, and Leah

Teachers who have the ability to conduct research and use the findings to develop solutions to issues that plague education are worth their weight in gold. Derek used the data from research he conducted in graduate school to debate the testimony of a state senator and defeat the passage of a bill that would have had a negative effect on schools in his state for decades. The research provided him with the confidence he needed to take a stand. As a teacher leader, he understood how to apply the data from his study to real-life situations at school. Like many teachers, Derek had years of class-room experience. Having the ability to couple his teaching expertise with hard data from his research study was a game changer.

Research can do the same for you. Teachers are well-respected members of their communities, although most have little knowledge of how to conduct research and collect and utilize data to help elevate the profession. Derek's story is a perfect example of the effect research can have in the hands of a well-informed teacher.

Think about programs or protocols in your district that are in dire need of change. Solid research may be the lever you need to help things move forward. That was definitely the case for Daniele. She worked with a colleague to uncover a serious issue. They also used the research to develop a possible solution. According to Daniele,

> We had the data to say [that] something needed to change. Another teacher and I went to our principal and asked if we could have the autonomy to try something different. He agreed. Together, we developed a plan for the creation of a new class just for that group of boys. We changed everything. I added new forms of seating like bean bags [chairs] to my classroom. We created learning centers and flipped our instruction. The two of us developed a series of instructional videos the students could watch on their own time. We used class time to solve problems and work on projects. The goal was to ensure the students became vested partners in the learning process. Students were required to strengthen and develop their math vocabularies. They used those tools when explaining answers or asking questions. It wasn't enough for them to say, "I have a problem." We wanted to know what the problem was and how it needed to be addressed. The students used the videos and other resources to strengthen their content knowledge and develop confidence.
>
> The special education teachers and paraprofessionals were integrated into the classroom, as Algebra I is a required course. Many of them were reticent at first, as math wasn't their strong point. I said, "Don't worry. You can watch the videos and participate in class as well." That was the turning point.
>
> It took a while for the students to own the responsibility of going home and watching the videos. I had to help them fall back in love with learning

and with math. I had to make it consumable instead of a brick wall. We moved to mastery learning. The students had to get a 70 or better to move on. We always defaulted back to the data to show what the students were mastering and the rate of progression at which they were doing so. I communicated constantly with my principal and used different forms of data to help him understand the impact the class had on the students. In addition to test scores, information about how many parents had signed up to serve as volunteers, a drop in absences, and a reduction in discipline issues served as strong arguments to both administration and my colleagues that it was not just a room filled with chaos.

The success of the program led us to start a freshman academy. We built a team of the freshman teachers and discussed how we could improve the transition from middle school to high school. Our group went from 2 teachers to 15 because of the collegial relationships my colleague and I built and the data we shared. Some people think data is only about those hard numbers. I completely disagree. I think a data point is about the relationships you build to focus on the whole child. Data isn't just about the numbers. It's about the humanization of the numbers. That concept is how teacher leaders help move others from good to great.

Likewise, Leah used data to inform the United States Department of Education about the impact federal policy had on the profession. Leah didn't stop there. The experience of sharing qualitative research as a teacher ambassador for the U.S. Department of Education opened another door. Here's how Leah describes her experience:

As fellows, we were encouraged to contact our state superintendent and share what we had learned. That wasn't easy. I didn't get a response right away. It took three or four times before I finally received an invitation to present to the state superintendent and his cabinet. They gave me 30 minutes. I filled an hour sharing my experience. At the end of the meeting, he invited me to form and facilitate an advisory council for Wisconsin. I had the ability to take the federal model and use it to create a conduit to funnel stories about students and teachers from across Wisconsin directly to the Department of Public Instruction. We still meet three times each year.

I learned that no matter what your political stance, children are a common ground that we can all agree on. My goal is to ensure the small voice is not forgotten. I teach in one of the counties with the highest poverty rates in the state. We used to do manufacturing. Those jobs are gone, and the family farms are closing. I tell people to be truthful about the stories they tell. Focus on the genuine real-life stories and less about the numbers. My experience at the state and federal level provided me with the opportunity to share the real stories of students and teachers from around the state. They help me to advocate for the people who are doing one of the hardest jobs in the world.

Teacher leaders are just starting to understand how to collect, package, and use data in order to improve instruction and transform the educational landscape. A study from ACT (Dougherty, 2015) suggests that discussions on data need to be part of a teacher's regular routine. Jennifer Morrison (2008–2009) explains the mind shifts teachers must undergo in order to do this successfully:

> Although coaching teachers in using data helps them feel less overwhelmed by it, if teachers are ever to use data powerfully, they must become coaches, helping themselves and colleagues draw on data to guide student learning, find answers to important questions, and analyze and reflect together on teaching practice.

Daniele, Derek, and Leah were confronted with complex issues. However, all three of them used data to isolate a problem, develop long-term solutions, and inform others along the way. As a teacher leader, look for ways to integrate conversations on data into department and grade-level meetings in order to grow your team's confidence in how to analyze data to shape instruction. Research and data can become your new best friends and assist in the transformation of your school.

5

Staking Your Claim: Using Advocacy to Amplify Your Voice, Strengthen the Profession, and Drive Change

When the whole world is silent, even one voice becomes powerful.

—Malala Yousafzai

Soon after Michael Dunlea was recognized for his excellence in teaching as a finalist for New Jersey Teacher of the Year for 2012, he faced a teacher's worst nightmare—a standoff with the superintendent. A second-career educator and National Board–certified teacher, Michael had implemented project-based learning and a challenging, differentiated curriculum for elementary school kids that was the talk of his community. The school had a waiting list of families who wanted their children to be in Mr. Dunlea's class. At the same time, a wave of conformity swept across his district, requiring all teachers to use identical programs with identical pacing regardless of the wonderful learning experiences that were already happening in classrooms across the city. Teachers were written up if the student work posted in the hallways had errors, if they were teaching phonics in isolation, or if they used worksheets. Instead of showing teachers how to improve, the district used an approach that emphasized micromanagement and strict adherence to regulations. The climate began to demoralize a lot of very good teachers, and the children were definitely suffering. Michael knew he had to do the unthinkable —confront those who were in charge in the hope of making change.

When Allison Riddle was named Utah's 2014 Teacher of the Year, she traveled all over the state representing teachers. In her travels, she was struck by the inequities she discovered. Some schools were flush with enthusiastic, brilliant teachers and beautiful, stimulating spaces, whereas others withered under the weight of a lack of working facilities and teachers who were demoralized—or worse, who had low expectations for kids, their profession, and the future. In some cities, teachers were expertly led, and a sense of enthusiasm and professionalism reigned. Sadly, in too many places with different budget realities, she saw that teachers and kids were suffering. Someone needed to fight to make sure that every child and every teacher were able to have a quality school experience. Someone needed to speak up and out on behalf of Utah's educators.

Joe was recognized in 2007 as the Illinois Teacher of the Year. The opportunity provided him with the ability to connect with other State Teachers of the Year (STOYs) from around the country as part of the National Teacher of the Year program sponsored by the Council of Chief State School Officers (CCSSO). For decades, most STOYs returned to the classroom after their year was over and the next class was named. From that point forward, there was little opportunity for the STOYs to use their newfound skills to advocate for the profession as a collective group. By 2007, more than 2,000 teachers had been recognized as State Teachers of the Year since the inception of the program. However, most continued to work in isolation. They remained one of the greatest untapped educational resources in the United States. Joe and a cadre of his STOY classmates were determined to change the paradigm and create a space where those teachers could work together to transform public education.

The experiences of Michael, Allison, and Joe lead us to ask whether you have ever thought, "If they let teachers be in charge for even a little bit, a whole bunch of different, smarter decisions might get made." If your answer is yes, you aren't alone. For so many teachers, an array of new programs, policies, and initiatives are handed down from above with little, if any, input from the professionals most directly affected by them. Instead, important decisions about working conditions, curriculum, or even compensation are made without teachers ever having a seat at the table.

Here's an example. In 2010, a school district on the West Coast implemented a Breakfast in the Classroom program to ensure that all students started school ready to learn (Klein, 2013). Nearly 80 percent of all students in the district are eligible for free or reduced meals, but fewer than 29 percent of students were participating in the school breakfast program served in the cafeteria. Finding a way to get healthy, nutritious meals to the students who need it most was an obvious problem in search of a solution. If students weren't willing to go to the cafeteria before school to receive their breakfast, then breakfast would be brought to them—in the classroom. On the surface, this decision sounds like a smart and thoughtful solution, except for one thing. Few, if any, teachers were consulted on how to implement the initiative in ways that thoughtfully considered the real impact on the classroom.

From the reduction in instructional minutes to the increase in classroom pest and rodent populations, a great idea quickly became one fraught with real logistical challenges for the teachers tasked with front-line implementation. There were the messes that serving breakfast created, the disruptions caused by late students who still needed to be fed, storage and waste issues, and increased personal spending by teachers on cleaning supplies. In short, the program had created a quandary. Because solutions to these issues weren't presented up front, frustrations boiled over at many schools, seemingly pitting teachers against a program designed to help the people they cared about most: children. All of this could have been avoided if teachers had been at the table where decisions like this get made.

But having a seat at the table to advocate for educators is a foreign concept for most of us. It can be an intimidating one as well. First, the sheer number of hours it takes to be a competent teacher is daunting. There often aren't enough hours in the day to accomplish all that needs to be done, much less attend to advocacy work. Second, learning to advocate for teachers requires a comprehensive understanding of the issues that confront us in our own buildings, our districts, and our states. Third, it's safe to say that the kind of person who wanted to become a teacher might not also enjoy developing the skills required to stand up and engage in activism on behalf of the profession. The research, the public-speaking skills, and the ability to articulate a message and push for solutions with stakeholders add up to something more akin to what we might expect from political scientists, activists, or—gasp!—politicians.

And yet, as the famous saying goes, if teachers aren't at the table, we are often on the menu. If we hope to be the change we wish to see in education, then we can't wait for some magical cavalry to ride in and save the day. We *are* the cavalry, but we have not been as vocal, as organized, or as empowered as we need to be if we hope to make real and lasting changes.

Strategies for Using Advocacy to Elevate the Profession

What our cavalry has going for us is that we teachers are allergic to the word *no*. We are constantly looking for ways for everyone to succeed to the best of their ability. We thrive on win-win situations. Applying a teacher's attitude and way of thinking to the challenges that face education can lead to an abundance of creative, innovative, and workable solutions. Combined with the legislative know-how of policymakers, the potential strength of teachers' advocacy is unstoppable. In this chapter, we share several strategies for how to use your voice and your enormous professional authority to strengthen and improve the profession.

Go Looking for Problems

All professional activism in education begins when teachers notice something they wish were done differently and better. Whether it's being asked to teach a new curriculum without any training or noticing that a schoolwide reading program is disproportionately hurting struggling students, there are times when teachers realize they must speak up.

If you're in this situation, it's typical to start by finding workable, fair solutions for yourself so that you can continue serving your own students in the best way possible. Then, reach out to colleagues to see who else may be similarly affected. When you discover that others share your concerns, come together and brainstorm solutions. Share what you've tried and listen to how others are handling the situation. Come up with a series of plans for how to repair, redesign, or remove programs, policies, or protocols that are hurting kids and teachers.

Combine Facts and Human Stories to Develop Effective Advocacy

No matter what the issues are, teachers who engage in advocacy work find that the most persuasive arguments are those that combine raw facts and data with the human faces and stories of those who are affected. This means you need to do your homework before you pick up the phone, write that op-ed piece, or knock on a senator's door. But do not fear! As a teacher, you occupy a uniquely powerful position that gives you access to scads of data points and the names and faces of children whose lived realities are harmed and helped by decisions made far from the classroom.

Gather all the facts you can about the problem you are confronting, and be ready to answer the tough questions about your data. Don't enter an advocacy conversation with personal anecdotes unless you have plenty of data to show that your issue is broader than decision makers realize. Whenever possible, lead with a story; then, link every data point you deliver to a real student or teacher who is affected. Many state and local decision makers don't ever see or know what happens to actual students and teachers when they write new laws or implement sweeping new policies. They tend to respond to real-life stories about the impact their decisions have. It's imperative, then, to bring honest accounts to their attention if you hope to sway hearts and minds.

Always Come Prepared with a Plan

Principals and school leaders of all types are tasked with making hundreds of decisions as they try to steer the complex organization that is a school. They also hear more than a fair number of complaints. Complaining is easy, and far too many teachers do it without backing up their complaints with workable, thoughtful ideas—or even the willingness to brainstorm solutions with school leadership. They expect someone else to do the leg work to solve their problems.

As teacher leaders, we handle these situations differently. We know that our bosses are busy people who want the best for teachers and kids and appreciate educators who take the time to research a problem and prepare possible solutions before making a concern known. We know they want to say yes to solutions that make sense and that make teaching and learning better for everyone.

When you want to see change happen at your school, it's imperative that you bring your school leaders a workable pathway for accomplishing that change and commit yourself to helping see it through. Be ready to do a lot of the work yourself initially, with others jumping in once you get approval. Begin, though, by creating a win-win scenario for leaders to sign off on. Once you have been given a green light, hit the gas and go.

A plan was exactly what Joe and his fellow 2007 State Teachers of the Year needed to help move their initiative forward. The CCSSO had invited the class to assemble for the first time in January 2007 in Dallas, Texas. It was there that the STOYs decided to organize so they could have a collective voice. In a hotel meeting room, they shared their thoughts on the responsibility they felt to protect the rights of students and teachers across the nation. That meeting of deeply committed teachers proved to be the beginning of a long, arduous effort to advance teacher leadership. It quickly became apparent that they needed a plan, and so they used every free second they had that week to meet repeatedly. By week's end, they had a rough outline of a plan to guide their actions. Over time, the plan evolved, but their initial roadmap helped guide their actions.

Set Aside Fear and Remember You're the Perfect Person for This Job

Sticking your neck out for something you believe in takes courage. It also requires *confrontation*. That word alone is enough to scare most teachers into inaction, but it needn't be that way. As a teacher, you are uniquely qualified to speak on anything related to schooling, pedagogy, child development, curriculum, and at least a dozen other education-related topics. You spend roughly 200 days a year immersed in the teaching profession, and you see how every law, every policy, and every decision affects your students. Standing up to face an issue that concerns you or your students and colleagues certainly requires bravery; but it also requires knowledge, expertise, solutions-oriented thinking, flexibility, and dedication. Didn't those words just describe you? We thought so. When in doubt, remember: there is no one more qualified to speak on education issues than a teacher.

In 2012, a school board member in Michael Dunlea's district reached out to him to hear more about what was happening with teachers in his school. Michael was nervous. He knew how bad things had gotten, how low morale was, and how close to quitting many of his friends were. But he was conflicted. Speaking to the board meant going around his own leadership team. Even though he'd been frank with them about his own frustrations, he knew that he was now being asked to speak on behalf of all the teachers who felt as he did. Ethically, he wasn't sure if he would be crossing any lines or upsetting any established chain of command. He even wondered if he might lose his job. But something inside him told him that this moment was his chance to speak truth to power and tell those who were in a position to make a change why they should do so.

Joe can pinpoint the moment he and his colleagues turned this same kind of doubt about their authority into determination to lead. The 2007 STOYS were met with resentment and skepticism when they decided to organize. Some people struggled to understand what they were trying to accomplish. One policymaker said, "It's just a group of STOYs who have grown too big for their britches." It would have been easy for the group to give up; they had little outside support and no resources. None of them thought they were anything special. However, they were driven by the voices of the students and teachers they represented. They understood this was an opportunity to bring their stories to light on the national stage. At some point in the journey, they had to believe in themselves because no one else did.

Stay Informed

Teachers' day-to-day workloads make it tough to find time to read up on current issues in education—but doing so is necessary. Teacher leaders don't wait until policies made somewhere far away are affecting their classrooms; they know about them long before they land on the classroom doorstep.

There are several places you can go to get the information you need. Both the National Education Association and the American Federation of Teachers have websites with links to current policy and information about the positions and recommendations your union may have taken regarding those positions. But don't stop there. Continue on to your state department of education's website, as well as state clearinghouses, where you can find everything from payroll data, to information on hiring trends, to graduation rates. Attend your local district's board meetings and watch state board of education meetings online. The most important work to engage in at this stage is to gain a comprehensive understanding of why district leaders or elected officials are making certain policy decisions. To be an effective advocate, you need to know what's happening and why.

Open and Maintain Lines of Communication with Decision Makers

Learn who your site, local, state, and federal education policymakers are. Find out who works on education and budget committees at the state and national levels. Find out how local school budgets and governance work. You don't have to dive too deep to find out the basics about how education policy is developed, but do find out as much as you can. Learn how to contact decision makers so that you are easily able to initiate conversations around key issues that are important to you. Take advantage of any training available from your union or other professionals on the best protocols for engaging with decision makers.

Initially, reach out to introduce yourself, describe your work circumstances, and share any areas of focus you have in common with these power brokers. Keep the first contact light and breezy, but let them know you'd like to maintain a communication channel with them on education issues. By all means, invite them to your school to visit and see great teaching and learning in action. Whenever an opportunity arises to reach out, do so. Send congratulations and thanks to policymakers for working hard for kids. Send information on education topics coming up for debate by the board, in the state legislature, and in the U.S. House of Representatives or Senate. Offer to provide support or help on the issues you care most about and on which a teacher leader's voice and experience could be helpful to them. Understand as best you can what it is policymakers need or wish to know from teachers on the front lines, and tailor your messaging to meet those needs. You might find legislators using your examples or information to make points with their colleagues. Once you have a line of communication open and maintained, it's much easier to engage in the important dialogue of advocacy when the time comes.

The importance of developing strong communication lines became apparent to Joe and his STOY cohort as soon as they left their first gathering. In those days, social media platforms were just beginning to emerge. Joe and his colleagues used e-mail and online bulletin boards to share information. People were assigned roles to help ensure project deadlines were met. The group used Sunday evening conference calls to develop a plan and hone their pitches to policymakers and teacher groups.

Build the Pitch

When you have the undivided attention of someone who can effect the change you want to see in education, be prepared with a concise and potent statement of your wishes or needs, along with a solution. Commonly called the "elevator pitch," this statement is the vehicle you can use to initiate dialogue with key decision makers. Your pitch should be about 30–60 seconds long; it should contain a statement of the problem, some of the outcomes you've seen firsthand, a reason why changes are needed, and some ideas about a solution you'd like to see.

Nailing this pitch is vital, so revise it, refine it, and practice it with your colleagues and others until you can give it in your sleep. It must be articulate, direct, and positive. It needs to capture the attention of decision makers and give them three things: a sense of the problem, a sense of your qualifications to discuss and potentially help solve this problem, and a way to work toward a solution. You should be able to deliver this pitch calmly and confidently and with an ease that demonstrates your skill and professionalism.

These are tough standards to meet, we know, but you will get few chances to make your case and probably even fewer minutes to do it. The goal is to deliver a pitch that will invite future dialogue. And make sure you have business cards with updated contact information handy to pass out once you're done with the pitch. There's nothing worse than ending strong only to have a policymaker turn to leave and ask, "How can I reach you?" while you run behind, scribbling your e-mail address on a piece of scrap paper. End your interaction by handing over your business card and asking if you can continue the conversation at a later time. Offer to reach out in a day or so, and then follow up. When you follow up, repeat your name and school, remind the person of the conversation you had earlier, and go from there.

Here's a sample pitch Rebecca used recently when speaking with representatives of a California state senator on the topic of teacher tenure:

> Good afternoon. I was hoping to talk with you about the upcoming senate bill on teacher tenure and the "last in, first out" (LIFO) provisions within California's policy. I've been working closely with several new teachers, and they are some of the most dedicated, enthusiastic, excellent teachers I have ever worked with. They are changing kids' lives every single day. Yet, if this bill passes, and if LIFO is retained, they will be pink-slipped first. For my colleague Angela, this will be her fourth pink slip simply because she is a new teacher without the years of seniority my veteran colleagues enjoy. It's devastating to see someone as hardworking as she is get shown the door, when teachers who have long ago lost their zeal for teaching, their love for kids, and their effectiveness get to keep their jobs simply because they've been at it longer. There must be a way to encourage teachers to stay in the profession, but to also stay strong in their work. I would love an opportunity to talk with you about how to remove the last in, first out provisions from the senate bill in favor of more logical policies that leverage teacher quality and honor the best of us. When might you be able to discuss this?

Learn How to Amplify Your Voice

A single, passionate, well-informed voice can pack plenty of power. However, there is also tremendous power in numbers. You can partner with several groups and organizations to learn how to engage in advocacy work. They can help put you in contact with decision makers in places where your advocacy work can have the greatest impact. Start with your union. Typically, unions have pathways you can follow to your state capital to lobby legislators on issues of vital importance. They host listening sessions to learn about various bills being submitted for votes and what teachers' positions on those issues should be. These meetings are designed to train and prepare teachers to discuss policy issues and implications with their representatives. You can learn about the process by which a bill becomes law and how to engage meaningfully with lawmakers.

There are dozens, if not hundreds, of other teacher advocacy groups doing similar work in states nationwide, such as the National Network of State Teachers of the Year (NNSTOY), the Hope Street Group, the Association of American Educators, Teach Plus, Educators for Excellence, ASCD, and several content-specific associations that all advocate on behalf of educators, using teacher voices to do so. Find a group whose purpose matches your goal and add your voice to theirs. The result may be change that is more powerful than what you could do on your own.

Allison Riddle took on just such a task by creating a group of passionate, engaged teachers to address some of the issues she saw across Utah when she was her state's teacher of the year. Through her contacts and affiliation with NNSTOY, Allison and other former teachers of the year formed their own state chapter, the Utah State Teachers of the Year (USTOY), to work on issues facing teachers and to advocate for solutions. She and her colleagues faced their first major challenge fairly soon after they formed their chapter. Here's her account:

> In the summer of 2016, our state legislature issued a ruling that created a level-one teacher license where prospective teachers could earn licensure

with a bachelor's degree and a passing score on a subject-specific Praxis exam. No pedagogical training of any kind was required before a newly licensed teacher could enter a classroom and begin teaching. Everyone in our USTOY group thought that was nuts. Together, we crafted a letter to our state representatives and state school board that was deeply passionate about why we felt this was a bad idea. We all knew that doing the job of teacher well is spectacularly difficult even when we are educated and trained well. Imagining the problems that would arise in classrooms with untrained laymen responsible for the health, welfare, and achievement of their students was not insignificant.

We signed and sent the letter from our group, and each individual USTOY member's [name was] on the letter, but because the letter was sent from my e-mail address, I received a call almost immediately from three different state board of education members. I was kind of shocked at how fast we got a response. Each asked me if I was a Utah Education Association Member, and I said yes and clarified that I was writing on behalf of more than just my union, but for myself and my colleagues in USTOY who have been recognized for their distinguished classroom practice. As soon as they knew I wasn't going to be spouting a canned party line from the union, they said, "Let's talk."

Advocacy Pitfalls and How to Avoid Them

Unless you have studied political science in school or have an intimate knowledge of how governance works, chances are you're a neophyte like us when it comes to advocacy work beyond the classroom. Many teachers have had to stump for funding or advocate for a program on our campuses, and somehow, that feels easy. But how many of us truly feel at home calling a politician or writing an impassioned op-ed for the papers? Probably not many. What might surprise you is how deeply our realities and the stories we share about our work can influence policymaking. In the sections that follow, learn what steps you can take to develop your own approach to educator activism.

Assuming Policymakers Are Against Teachers

Teachers tend to doubt their ability to effectively advocate for changes in education policy (Hinnant-Crawford, 2016). Although this view is not surprising in a divisive political climate, one of the worst mistakes a teacher leader can make when approaching policymakers is to adopt an "us-versus-them" mentality. The conversation doesn't have to look like a boxing match that pits practitioners against policymakers.

Instead, consider taking a different approach. Consider the fact that, like most teachers, policymakers are typically good people who have dedicated their lives to public service because they want to make a difference. In addition, the vast majority of them want to hear from you. Unfortunately, communication channels between teachers and policymakers are practically nonexistent. One of your jobs as a teacher leader is to build one. School board members, state legislators, and congressional leaders are only a phone call away. Spend a little time doing your due diligence and conduct a deep dive to learn more about the people who represent you. Your union can be extremely helpful in this process. Union leaders are generally well informed and can provide a lot of background information on policymakers from the local to national level. The next step is yours.

Before making a call, create an outline that helps identify the questions that you want answered. It's likely that you will be able to speak directly to local and state policymakers, but don't be frustrated if your congressional leaders don't pick up the phone on the first ring. In fact, it may be very difficult to have a direct conversation with one of them. Don't jump to the conclusion that they don't want to hear from you. Instead, ask for the aide who is in charge of the particular topic you want to discuss. Aides do a tremendous amount of work at the Capitol and are responsible for ensuring that your concerns are shared with your U.S. representative or senator. While you are on the phone, don't forget to ask when the representative or senator will be in your area and invite him or her to come to your school. Many of them have a strong interest in the schools in their district and are more than happy to meet with you and your students.

As with any relationship, it takes time to build trust. The conduit you create with policymakers is vital as it provides them with a direct pipeline to the school and helps them develop a deeper understanding of the effect that policy has on student achievement and the profession.

Presenting Problems with No Solutions or Willingness to Brainstorm Ideas

A surefire way to kill your advocacy effort is to spend your time focusing on problems instead of solutions. At first glance, that statement might appear like some sort of trivial play on words. It's not. Advocacy can be extremely hard work. Depending on the situation, progress may be difficult to identify. It's times like those when a positive mindset may be the only thing that keeps your team moving forward. Keeping a positive mindset doesn't mean ignoring the problems that you are facing. However, you are at risk of falling into a bottomless pit of negativity if all you ever see are problems. Instead, work with your teammates to generate a list of possible solutions. Solutions are extremely important for two reasons: they provide a way out and help generate feelings of hope.

For Joe, the farther he and his STOY colleagues went down the road, the more difficult the journey became. It would have been very easy for the team to have wallowed in self-pity because they couldn't find a sustainable funding source. However, the team worked really hard to stay focused on achieving their dream. In it, they saw a vehicle that could be used to help transform public education. The synergy from the group conversations drove them forward. They became solution oriented, and that is why they eventually found success.

Introducing Unnecessary Complexity

Don't get caught up in the mindset that bigger is better. If there is a simple solution that will help solve your problem, use it. The education world is notorious for making things more complicated than they need to be. Be careful of falling into the same trap by adding more fluff than substance. Work with your team to brainstorm multiple solutions. Rank them in order of difficulty and ability to rectify the issue at hand. Have serious conversations as a team about which solution best meets your needs. Make sure that personal ownership of a solution does not cloud your team's vision. Keep the end goal in mind at all times.

Forgetting About the Union's Perspective

Unions are an important part of the educational system. Take time to visit with union leadership during your advocacy journey. You may be surprised to discover they have an abundance of resources that can assist you in your work. Likewise, don't be afraid to meet with union leadership to share any concerns you have and what problems you are trying to solve. They may have advice to offer. It's also possible that your perspective is completely different from theirs. That's OK too. However, in those instances, it can be helpful to know where the union stands, what backing is available, or if they oppose your work. The goal is not to create conflict, but to build relationships. It's also important to remember that you have the right to your opinion. Working with others can be a balancing act. Building an awareness of how your local union operates and what support it can provide can only help advocacy move forward.

Quitting Too Soon

Advocacy is a marathon, not a sprint. Developing a strategic plan in the early phases of your work will help you get to where you want to go. Be sure to include goals and a time line, but build in flexibility. Don't make your plan so rigid that it cannot handle the winds of change. Otherwise, be prepared for it to collapse during the first storm. Patience and a determined, positive attitude will see you through to success.

Also, understand there will be bumps and bruises along the way. That's OK. It's part of the process. However, finding an external thought partner who is knowledgeable in the subject matter and whom you can bounce ideas off of can help you avoid some of the growing pains that are associated with advocacy work. Look for someone who is encouraging but honest. The last thing you need is a person who is unwilling to tell you the truth. A reality check may be just what you need.

Lessons Learned by—and from—Michael, Allison, and Joe

Perhaps you noticed something in common about the stories of the three teachers featured in this chapter. For each of them, there came a moment when a situation in their work lives elicited an overwhelming call to action. This in itself isn't unusual, as teachers are typically caring, empathetic souls who want to make the world a better place. But even within this esteemed group, more teachers than you might think tell themselves, "Someone else will take care of this; it's not my job." Not so for teacher leaders. In fact, the moment they realize that no one is better equipped to act than they are *is* the moment they become the teacher leaders they are meant to be.

When Michael's work life became miserable, he knew he needed to confront the issues head-on. Having earned his National Board certification, he knew a thing or two about great teaching and learning practices for children. He explains,

> I'd been praised and awarded for my novel, effective, and creative teaching practices by the very administrators who were now handing the teachers at my school scripted program after program and penalizing them for not conforming. My first step was to trust my experience, my qualifications, and my instincts about the validity of this curricular approach. I scheduled a meeting with my principal to share my concerns and to advocate for change. Initially supportive, my principal made no substantive changes, leaving things to go from bad to worse as teacher friends began to rapidly burn out, cry at work, and watch their students suffer. I realized I had a choice: leave the school I loved or fight for it.

Michael learned that it was important that he had both the data and the human stories to make his points to the school board when they came looking for information about why the staff at his school were so dissatisfied. As he describes it,

> When I spoke to our school board member, I shared all of our stories and discussed the teachers' concerns. I was told the board understood our issues and they realized that students were not getting an optimal education.

Because I seemed to have a solid understanding of the problem, I was asked to organize the 225 teachers in my district. I began by creating a communication network using private messages via social media. Teachers began talking about what they were seeing and what they wished to happen. The teachers believed it was time to meet and have a vote of no confidence in our current administration. Before we did that, we decided to conduct a climate survey, and the data from the survey helped everyone gain better insight into the depth and severity of the situation. The teachers in my building thought [our school] was the den of discontent. In actuality, there were two other buildings whose staffs were far angrier and frustrated. Even our union executive team was caught off guard as to the degree of discontent. It was important that we had all of this information in one place before we took any next steps.

In hindsight, Michael learned that it's OK to be fearful of entering situations like this, but it's not OK to do nothing. He recognizes that summoning the courage to act is what made all the difference:

I won't forget the feeling of being brave enough to stand up, speak out, and use my voice to make change. It was a visceral image for me. When I stood up at the school board [meeting] to discuss what was happening to teachers and students at my school and the unanimous vote of no confidence in our leaders, it was at that moment when I truly became a leader and was leading. I had moved people forward. I had helped my fellow teachers become active and to find their voice. I assisted them in discovering the bravery deep inside themselves and to have the courage to stand up and say that our district was doing something wrong that was hurting children and teachers. The situation was incredibly hairy. I still have a stress response when I think and talk about it. Eventually, the superintendent resigned and a more reasonable set of curricular expectations was implemented.

It all came down to that one moment on the phone when someone in a position to do something asked me if I was willing to lead the charge. I could have easily passed the baton, but I didn't. Why? Because even though I was nervous, even though I was scared, the one thing I knew for sure was that I was qualified to speak about and for teachers. If not me, then who?

For Allison, learning how to effectively advocate for the teachers and schools she'd seen in her travels around Utah required that she educate herself on the relevant points and issues. Not only did she need to have a firm grasp on the reasons for the inequities she'd seen; she also needed to know more about school funding and her state's budget. She needed to know who held the power positions in local and state government and how they worked to spend money, make policy, and pass legislation. She had to join with her advocacy groups to craft solutions and messaging around issues that mattered most and then learn to become a confident, articulate communicator of those messages. Many of us would find this prospect daunting, but not someone as doggedly determined as Allison was to make things better for teachers and kids.

She also learned how important it was to know her audience, to listen to their positions, and to have facts and figures at the ready when the time came to propose alternatives that might be suitable to both parties:

> First, I asked the legislators to tell me why they were so passionate about creating a shortcut to the classroom, and why they were committed to this bill. They explained that the ruling was designed to help fill a tremendous number of teacher vacancies in rural classrooms where students were sometimes being taught by substitutes for years at a time. After listening to their answers, I led into our position that pedagogical theory is vital and that these new hires needed to be immediately enrolled into a program of study that would provide this. Having consulted a variety of sources on the economic costs of hiring, training, and retaining teachers, I was able to find out the onboarding and induction costs for new hires. I used that data to share my understanding about the costs associated with hiring teachers who have no training and how that tends to add up once they are hired. When I shared this with the board members, I was quick to propose a solution where the costs connected to a level-one license would be spent to help ensure this fast-track [approach] resulted in teachers who were receiving the training and support necessary to be successful in the classroom.

> They were extremely responsive, I feel, because I listened to them and sought to understand their logic first. We had a much better conversation

because I knew what they were thinking and knew which direction to go with my answer and what to say to make them keep listening and to pitch what we felt was important. Our letter and these conversations were instrumental in having some language put into the bill that would call out special training for these level-one credential holders.

Finally, Allison and the USTOY group knew that once the advocacy door is open, it must remain open. The whole purpose of the work was to make sure teachers had a voice about the issues and decisions that most affected them. She advises others to do the same: work your connections, make the calls, and continue to lobby for what's important. As she describes it,

> Our initial foray into this level of advocacy was only the beginning. We continued to work together to push what we knew was important: recognizing teacher leadership and teacher efficacy. In our state, the concept of teacher leadership wasn't just foreign; it didn't exist. Sure, there were teachers in every school across the state working on leadership initiatives at their schools or in their teaching field, but our state had not recognized that title or idea formally. We knew we needed to do something about that.
>
> I made two appointments with my deputy state superintendent of schools, Syd Dixon. I brought in the NNSTOY white paper *The Right Trajectory*, which outlines potential and powerful pathways excellent teachers should be able to travel in their teaching careers. Our goal was to have the state of Utah recognize teacher leadership. [That goal] seems small at first, but in order for there to be future study, opportunities, funding, education, first a thing has to be recognized officially.
>
> It took our sustained efforts, information, and openness to cultivate a relationship with policymakers and to present our goals, but eventually we were successful. Last year, Senator Ann Millner, along with State Superintendent Syd Dixon, passed a bill defining teacher leadership. I know that our success came from our commitment to developing solid relationships and a willingness to understand the issues and their positions on them.

Joe and the STOY Class of 2007 can attest to the angst of advocacy. Slowly, one by one, members of their group started to fall off the calls and return their attention to things at home. It looked for a while like the status quo had won. However, a small group of STOYs continued to meet regularly for years. One door after another was shut in their faces. However, they remained positive and used those experiences to learn. Along the way, they continued to meet with policymakers and other educational stakeholders to share their dream. What Joe eventually discovered was that he and his colleagues were using those experiences to build a strong foundation. As time passed, they continued to practice and hone the pitch. Joe learned that it is important to look for opportunities as an advocate. Rarely do opportunities seek people out. Instead, teachers have to be willing to turn over every stone, follow every lead, and be prepared to share their pitch on a moment's notice. Joe's opportunity came at a meeting in Washington, D.C.

During the summer of 2010, the Bill and Melinda Gates Foundation was forming a committee to discuss what constituted meaningful professional development. Joe was invited to join the committee. It was there he met a program officer for the foundation, who happened to be seated next to him at dinner one evening. He took that opportunity to share his pitch. She was intrigued enough to extend an invitation for Joe to submit a proposal for an exploratory grant. Joe received the official acceptance letter a few weeks later.

The grant provided Joe with the funding to bring together a group of key stakeholders to discuss the feasibility of using the framework of the National State Teachers of the Year (NSTOY) to build an organization that focused on policy, practice, and advocacy. The convening was held later that summer in Chicago. The leadership team from NSTOY, the head of the National Teacher of the Year program from CCSSO, several STOYs (including the small team from the Class of 2007), the program officer from the Gates Foundation, and other key stakeholders were invited to attend.

During the two-day event, the STOYs painted a vivid picture of the current landscape and how NSTOY could assist in ensuring that teachers from across the country had the opportunity to help transform public education. Everyone walked away inspired. Good news followed a few months later when the Gates Foundation offered to support the project. Years of hard work and sacrifice had paid off. NSTOY eventually became NNSTOY (the National Network of State Teachers of the Year). It did not take long for others to recognize the value of NNSTOY. The phone started ringing with opportunities as soon as the doors were finally open.

Conclusion: It's Time to Set Out on Your Adventure

*You cannot discover new oceans unless you have the courage to
lose sight of the shore.*

—André Gide

Nestled within each amazing teacher is an urge. Maybe yours is small and
quiet, gently propelling you forward in your work. Maybe it's loud and insis-
tent and spills over into everything you do. It's the urge that repeatedly asks,
"What else? What more might I try with my students? What other wonderful things can my colleagues and I do for our kids?"

This impulse is the one that drives us to get better every day. Not every
teacher kindles this urge, but those who do are truly remarkable. In this book
you met 15 of them, 15 teachers who utterly and unapologetically love teaching but who wanted something more. They wanted better lessons, better relationships with their colleagues, better learning experiences for themselves,
better opportunities for kids, and better schools for their communities. Most
important, they wanted a stronger teaching profession that accurately represented the challenging, exciting realities of the American classroom.

Did they wait for someone else to design this transformation and deliver
it to their doorstep? No. They took matters into their own hands and set out
to make the change they wished to see. Their successes, each unique, are

remaking what education looks like and is like for teachers all over the country. Their stories help us piece together a rough map of what teacher leadership looks like and the myriad directions that this work may take. Although each of them traveled their own route, deep within each one was that same urge and that same voice that whispers, "What else?"

We hope that reading the examples of others will give you the confidence to listen to your own inner voice and set out on a journey to change your education workplace. But following their lead requires more than just this map of where they've been. You'll need to pack courage and belief for your journey as well.

For so long, the only way for teachers to move up in their profession was to move out of the classroom. If they wanted to lead others, the pathway would take them away from the students they love. How dispiriting to know that they would have to sacrifice the very thing that drew them to teaching in order to strengthen their profession. Many have had to swallow that sadness and disappointment and rely on the belief that somehow, in other necessary ways, they were doing important work that mattered. We believe, as do these 15 teachers, that those days are truly over.

Teachers all over the United States are gathering the courage to ask for opportunities to work on projects that will help their kids and their schools without leaving the classroom. They are asking for a voice in the conversation and a seat at the table, and they're getting it. This effort takes courage, but courage is something all great teachers have. You have it too. Are you ready to locate and activate yours?

You'll need courage to know that your journey and destination may not always be clear. You might not know exactly how to get started, or what might result from your endeavors. Go anyway.

It's not about asking permission to do something, or being able to plot out every possible wrinkle in your itinerary or say with certainty what will be different once you are done. It's about having the bravery to try something you haven't done before but you know needs to be done.

You will find quite quickly that being a teacher leader is foreign territory and sometimes intimidating. Unlike the experience of teaching with a tight lesson plan, things can and do go awry. That's all right. You have the skills, the mindset, the patience, and the passion to find a way through to solutions. But if you don't have the courage to begin, you'll never know how amazing you might be at this incredibly necessary work.

Knitted tight to your courage must be an unwavering belief in your expertise, your authority, and your value as an educator. Remind yourself that you have all the tools you need to be successful at leading in this arena. First, you have incredible professional expertise. On a daily basis, you make thousands of decisions about and for your students' learning. You know the latest theories and research, and you employ those understandings every day that you do this work.

Second, you have one of the most important jobs in the world. Education is the profession that makes all others possible. Never say you're "just" a teacher. Proclaim it proudly, and never qualify the declaration or speak about teaching as if it doesn't measure up to other professions.

Third, you have the moral authority to step up and say what should and should not happen to the people who do this work for children. There is *no one else* more qualified, more respected, or more able to make decisions in this space than teachers.

Fourth, as a teacher, you have powerful, front-line stories to tell about how policies and practices imposed on teachers dramatically affect children. If you want to see how education is working anywhere, ask teachers. They can tell you. And those stories are what move hearts and minds in the right direction. It's imperative that you gather such stories and use them to advocate for all teachers.

Finally, as a teacher, you are a solutions-oriented yes person. You are always looking for ways for everyone to succeed to the best of their ability and potential. You thrive on win-win situations. When you put that attitude to the challenges that face education, a great number of creative, innovative, and workable solutions are possible.

For these reasons, and a dozen more, you must believe that *you* are the perfect person to do this work. There isn't anyone better, more knowledgeable, harder working, or more invested in success than a teacher who wishes to lead.

You may have been motivated to read this book because you were interested but unsure of how to become a teacher leader. Perhaps you have watched others take this pathway and wanted it for yourself. For whatever reason, we hope that the stories and advice contained within these pages have assured you of just how much you have in common with the intrepid travelers already on the road.

By now, you've learned more about what skills and tools you'll need. You've seen how the things that make great teachers also make great teacher leaders, and that you have those same abilities. You now know that you're not alone. There are thousands of others fighting for more and better experiences for children, for teachers, and for the education community at large.

We invite you to join us and be part of the movement to make a better world, one child at a time, one classroom at a time, one school at a time.

All you need to do is choose your adventure.

References

Asia Society. (2015). *Implementing highly effective teacher policy and practice: The 2015 international summit on the teaching profession* [Report]. Retrieved from https://asiasociety.org/global-cities-education-network/implementing-highly-effective-teacher-policy-and-practice

Baepler, P., Walker, J. D., & Driessen, M. (2014). It's not about seat time: Blending, flipping, and efficiency in active learning classrooms. *Computers & Education, 78*, 227–236. doi: 10.1016/j.compedu.2014.06.006

Barth, R. S. (2004). *Learning by heart*. San Francisco: Jossey-Bass.

Behrstock, E., & Clifford, M. (2009, February). *Leading Gen Y teachers: Emerging strategies for school leaders.* Washington, DC: National Comprehensive Center for Teacher Quality. Retrieved from https://gtlcenter.org/sites/default/files/docs/February2009Brief.pdf

Behrstock-Sherratt, E., Bassett, K., Olson, D., & Jacques, C. (2014). *From good to great: Exemplary teachers share perspectives on increasing teacher effectiveness across the career continuum.* Washington, DC: National Network of State Teachers of the Year. Retrieved from http://www.nnstoy.org/publications/from-good-to-great-exemplary-teachers-share-perspectives-on-increasing-teacher-effectiveness-across-the-career-continuum/

Burton, T. (2015). *Exploring the impact of teacher collaboration on teacher learning and development* [Doctoral dissertation]. Retrieved from http://scholarcommons.sc.edu/etd/3107

Catmull, E., with Wallace, A. (2014). *Creativity, Inc.: Overcoming the unseen forces that stand in the way of true inspiration*. New York: Random House.

Crouch, D. (2015, June 17). Highly trained, respected and free: Why Finland's teachers are different. *The Guardian*. Retrieved from https://www.theguardian.com/education/2015/jun/17/highly-trained-respected-and-free-why-finlands-teachers-are-different

Danielson, C. (2009). *Talk about teaching: Leading professional conversations.* Thousand Oaks, CA: Corwin, National Association of Secondary School Principals, and National Staff Development Council.

Darling-Hammond, L., Hyler, M. E., & Gardner, M. (2017). *Effective teacher professional development.* Palo Alto, CA: Learning Policy Institute.

Dediu, A. (2015). *Tall poppy syndrome and its effect on work performance* [Master's dissertation]. Christchurch, NZ: University of Canterbury. Retrieved from https://ir.canterbury.ac.nz/bitstream/handle/10092/10261/Anna-Dediu-Dissertation.pdf?sequence=1&isAllowed=y

Dougherty, C. (2015). *How school district leaders can support the use of data to improve teaching and learning* [Policy brief]. ACT Research and Policy. Retrieved from www.act.org/content/dam/act/unsecured/documents/Use-of-Data.pdf

Dreyfus, S. E., & Dreyfus, H. L. (1980). *A five-stage model of the mental activities involved in directed skill acquisition.* Berkeley, CA: University of California, Berkeley.

Dweck, C. S. (2008). *Mindset: The new psychology of success.* New York: Ballantine Books.

Goodwin, B., & Miller, K. (2013). Research says evidence on flipped classrooms is still coming in. *Educational Leadership, 70*(6), 78–80. Retrieved from http://www.ascd.org/publications/educational-leadership/mar13/vol70/num06/Evidence-on-Flipped-Classrooms-Is-Still-Coming-In.aspx

Hattie, J. (2012). *Visible learning for teachers: Maximizing impact on learning.* New York: Routledge.

Hinnant-Crawford, B. (2016). Education policy influences efficacy: Teacher beliefs in their ability to change education policy. *International Journal of Teacher Leadership, 7*(2), 1–27. Retrieved from https://eric.ed.gov/?id=EJ1137496

Ingersoll, R. M. (2003). *Who controls teachers' work?* Cambridge, MA: Harvard University Press.

Ingersoll, R. M. (2012, May 16). Beginning teacher induction: What the data tell us. *Education Week.* Retrieved from https://www.edweek.org/ew/articles/2012/05/16/kappan_ingersoll.h31.html#

Jacques, C., Behrstock-Sherratt, E., Parker, A., & Bassett, K. (2017). *Investing in what it takes to move from good to great: Exemplary educators identify their most important learning experiences.* Washington, DC: National Network of State Teachers of the Year.

Jacques, C., Weber, G., Bosso, D., Olson, D., & Bassett, K. (2016). *Great to influential: Teacher leaders' roles in supporting instruction.* Washington, DC: National Network of State Teachers of the Year. Retrieved from http://www.nnstoy.org/publications/great-to-influential/

Johnson, S. M., Berg, J. H., & Donaldson, M. L. (2005). *Who stays in teaching and why: A review of the literature on teacher retention.* Boston: NRTA's Educator Support Network.

Katzenmeyer, M., & Moller, G. (2001). *Awakening the sleeping giant: Helping teachers develop as leaders.* Thousand Oaks, CA: Corwin.

Klein, K. (2013, April 29). The messy complications of breakfast in the classroom. *Los Angeles Times*. Retrieved from http://www.latimes.com/opinion/opinion-la/la-ol-lausd-breakfast-classroom-20130429-story.html

Knowles, M. (1970). *The modern practice of adult education: From pedagogy to andragogy.* Cambridge, UK: Cambridge University Press.

Kraft, M. A., & Dougherty, S. M. (2013). The effect of teacher-family communication on student engagement: Evidence from a randomized field experiment. *Journal of Research on Educational Effectiveness, 6*(3), 199–222.

Lipton, L., & Wellman, B. (2003). *Mentoring matters: A practical guide to learning-focused relationships* (2nd ed.). Arlington, MA: MiraVia.

Means, B., Chen, E., DeBarger, A., & Padilla, C. (2011). *Teachers' ability to use data to inform instruction: Challenges and supports.* Washington, DC: U.S. Department of Education, Office of Planning, Evaluation, and Policy Development. Retrieved from https://www.sri.com/sites/default/files/publications/teachers_ability_to_use_data_to_inform_instruction_challenges_and_supports.pdf

Morrison, J. (2008–2009). Why teachers must be data experts. *Educational Leadership, 66*(4). Retrieved from www.ascd.org/publications/educational-leadership/dec08/vol66/num04/Why-Teachers-Must-Be-Data-Experts.aspx

Nakane, J., & Hall, R. W. (2002). Ohno's method: Creating a survival work culture. *Target, 18*(1), 6–15. Wheeling, IL: Association for Manufacturing Excellence. Retrieved from www.ame.org/sites/default/files/target_articles/02-18-1-Ohnos_Method.pdf

National Center for Education Statistics. (2018). Back to school statistics. *Fast Facts.* Retrieved from https://nces.ed.gov/fastfacts/display.asp?id=372

National Commission on Excellence in Education. (1983). *A nation at risk: The imperative for educational reform: A report to the nation and the secretary of education.* Washington, DC: United States Department of Education.

National Commission on Teaching and America's Future. (2007). *The high cost of teacher turnover* [Policy brief]. Washington, DC: Author. Retrieved from nctaf.org/wp-content/uploads/NCTAFCostofTeacherTurnoverpolicybrief.pdf

O'Donnell, J., & Saker, A. (2018, March 19). Teen suicide is soaring. Do spotty mental health and addiction treatment share blame? *USA Today*. Retrieved from https://www.usatoday.com/story/news/politics/2018/03/19/teen-suicide-soaring-do-spotty-mental-health-and-addiction-treatment-share-blame/428148002/

Pounder, D. G. (Ed.). (1998). *Restructuring schools for collaboration: Promises and pitfalls.* Albany, NY: State University of New York Press.

Quintero, D., & Hansen, M. (2017, June 2). English learners and the growing need for qualified teachers. *Brown Center Chalkboard*. Retrieved from https://www.brookings.edu/blog/brown-center-chalkboard/2017/06/02/english-learners-and-the-growing-need-for-qualified-teachers/

Sinek, S. (2009). *How great leaders inspire action* [TED Talk]. Retrieved from https://www.ted.com/talks/simon_sinek_how_great_leaders_inspire_action

Smylie, M. A. (1992). Teachers' reports of their interactions with teacher leaders concerning classroom instruction. *Elementary School Journal, 93*(1), 85–98.

Smylie, M. A., Lazarus, V., & Brownlee-Conyers, J. (1996, Fall). Instructional outcomes of school-based participative decision making. *Education Evaluation & Policy Analysis, 18*(3), 181–198.

Teacher Leader Exploratory Consortium. (2011). *Teacher leader model standards*. Retrieved from http://www.teacherleaderstandards.org/

UNESCO Institute for Statistics. (2016). *The world needs almost 69 million new teachers to reach the 2030 education goals* [Policy brief]. Montreal, QC: Author. Retrieved from http://unesdoc.unesco.org/images/0024/002461/246124e.pdf

Index

About the Authors

Rebecca Mieliwocki has been an English teacher for more than 20 years and is the 2012 California and National Teacher of the Year. She was chosen from a group of 54 State Teachers of the Year to represent the United States' 3.2 million public school teachers in a year of travel, speaking, and advocacy that took her to 30 U.S. states and 10 nations.

In addition to teaching middle school English, Rebecca has taught high school composition and graduate-level education classes at California State University, Northridge. She is currently a teacher on special assignment with the Burbank Unified School District, where she coordinates secondary professional development and new teacher induction. In this capacity, she is responsible for onboarding new educators and helping them develop effective mindsets and professional dispositions that will stand them in good stead for their entire careers. She also oversees secondary-level instructional leadership teams, helping them to plan and execute personalized professional development for their colleagues.

Rebecca holds a bachelor of arts in speech communication from California Polytechnic State University and a master's degree in secondary English curriculum and instruction from the California State University, Northridge (CSUN). She is the 2005 California League of Middle Schools Educator of the Year for Southern California, a 2009 and 2013 PTA Honorary Service

Award Recipient, CSUN's 2013 Distinguished Alumni Award recipient, and the Zonta Club's Burbank Woman of the Year. She has served as a mentor for California's Beginning Teacher Support and Assessment (BTSA) induction program, a conference presenter, an author for the CSUN College of Education's Center for Teacher and Learning, and a contributing blogger for *EdWeek Teacher*. She has contributed to the national conversation on education through appearances and writing for *CBS This Morning*, CNN, *The Ellen Show*, PBS television, KPCC public radio, the *Los Angeles Times*, the *Sacramento Bee*, Phi Delta Kappa/Gallup Survey, and magazines including *Real Simple*, *Cosmopolitan*, Scholastic's *Instructor*, *Educational Horizons*, and *California Educator*. She can be reached at spellingcounts@att.net or on Twitter at @mrsmieliwocki.

Joseph Fatheree is an award-winning author, educator, and filmmaker. He has received numerous educational accolades, including being named one of the Top 10 Teachers in the World in 2016 by the Varkey Foundation. He is the 2007 Illinois Teacher of the Year and the 2009 recipient of the National Education Association's National Award for Teaching Excellence. He was a founding board member of Advance Illinois, an independent education advocacy and policy organization, and served as the director of strategic projects for the National Network of State Teachers of the Year (NNSTOY). Joseph is internationally recognized as a leader in technology integration, education policy, teacher leadership, innovation, global education, and curriculum design. He served on a professional development committee for the Bill and Melinda Gates Foundation and a curriculum advisory committee for ITVS/Independent Lens. He is also recognized as a Varkey Teacher Ambassador as part of the Global Teacher Prize.

Joseph's television work has aired nationally on PBS, the Documentary Channel, Hulu, and the Major League Baseball Network. As a producer he has received three Mid-America Emmy awards, two for producing and one for writing. He continues to serve as a full-time teacher at Effingham High School in Effingham, Illinois, where he teaches innovation in a classroom filled with student imagination, creativity, and a desire to change the world.

He can be reached at josephfatheree@gmail.com or on Twitter at @josephfatheree.

Katherine Bassett, MEd, is an education innovator and advocate who spent 26 years in the classroom as a middle school librarian and is New Jersey's 2000 State Teacher of the Year. She is currently the CEO of Tall Poppy (www.katherinebassett/tallpoppy), a consulting company founded to grow leaders through leadership research and professional learning, equity and bias awareness learning, and strengthened standards. She has also recently cofounded RAD Science (www.radssolution.com), focused on assessing social and emotional learning skills. She is the former president and CEO of the National Network of State Teachers of the Year. She served as director of policy and partnerships for the Center for Educator Effectiveness at Pearson, working to support research into educator practice and self-efficacy and to build partnerships with like-minded organizations. Formerly at Educational Testing Service, she led the development of certificates for library media and literacy for the National Board for Professional Teaching Standards, developed assessments of educator performance for six states, facilitated the work of a consortium to develop the Teacher Leader Model Standards, and served on the committees that revised the standards of the Interstate Teacher Assessment and Support Consortium (InTASC). She cofacilitated the development of the Model Code of Educator Ethics and has led the development of the Teacher Leadership Initiative for the National Education Association, the National Board for Professional Teaching Standards, and the Center for Teacher Quality. She can be reached at read12me@gmail.com or on Twitter at @read12me.

Related ASCD Resources

At the time of publication, the following resources were available (ASCD stock numbers appear in parentheses).

Print Products

The Artisan Teaching Model for Instructional Leadership: Working Together to Transform Your School by Kenneth Baum and David Krulwich (#116041)

Creating a Culture of Reflective Practice: Capacity-Building for Schoolwide Success by Pete Hall and Alisa Simeral (#117006)

Dream Team: A Practical Playbook to Help Innovative Educators Change Schools by Aaron Tait and Dave Faulkner (#119022)

Facilitating Teacher Teams and Authentic PLCs: The Human Side of Leading People, Protocols, and Practices by Daniel R. Venables (#117004)

Igniting Teacher Leadership: How do I empower my teachers to lead and learn? (ASCD Arias) by William Sterrett (#SF116039)

Leading Change Together: Developing Educator Capacity Within Schools and Systems by Eleanor Drago-Severson and Jessica Blum-DeStefano (#117027)

Leading in Sync: Teacher Leaders and Principals Working Together for Student Learning by Jill Harrison Berg (#118021)

Other Duties as Assigned: Tips, Tools, and Techniques for Expert Teacher Leadership by Jan Burgess and Donna Bates (#109075)

Reframing Teacher Leadership to Improve Your School by Douglas B. Reeves (#108012)

For up-to-date information about ASCD resources, go to www.ascd.org. You can search the complete archives of *Educational Leadership* at www.ascd.org/el.

PD Online

Building Teachers' Capacity for Success: Instructional Coaching Essentials by Pete Hall and Alisa Simeral (#PD15OC005M)

FIT Teaching in Action for Instructional Leaders by Nancy E. Frey, Stefani Hite, and Douglas B. Fisher (#PD17OC002M)

Leading Professional Learning: Building Capacity Through Teacher Leaders (#PD13OC010M)

ASCD myTeachSource®

Download resources from a professional learning platform with hundreds of research-based best practices and tools for your classroom at http://myteachsource.ascd.org/.

For more information, send an e-mail to member@ascd.org; call 1-800-933-2723 or 703-578-9600; send a fax to 703-575-5400; or write to Information Services, ASCD, 1703 N. Beauregard St., Alexandria, VA 22311-1714 USA.

WHOLE CHILD
TENETS

1 HEALTHY
Each student enters school
healthy and learns about and
practices a healthy lifestyle.

2 SAFE
Each student learns in an
environment that is physically
and emotionally safe for
students and adults.

3 ENGAGED
Each student is actively
engaged in learning and is
connected to the school and
broader community.

4 SUPPORTED
Each student has access to
personalized learning and is
supported by qualified,
caring adults.

5 CHALLENGED
Each student is challenged
academically and prepared
for success in college or
further study and for
employment and participation
in a global environment.

THE WHOLE CHILD

The ASCD Whole Child approach is an effort to transition from
a focus on narrowly defined academic achievement to one
that promotes the long-term development and success of all
children. Through this approach, ASCD supports educators,
families, community members, and policymakers as they move
from a vision about educating the whole child to
sustainable, collaborative actions.

Adventures in Teacher Leadership relates to the **engaged,
supported,** and **challenged** tenets.

*For more about the ASCD Whole Child approach,
visit **www.ascd.org/wholechild.***

Become an ASCD member today!
Go to www.ascd.org/joinascd
or call toll-free: 800-933-ASCD (2723)

ASCD
LEARN. TEACH. LEAD.